"Contentment may not be as e
thusiasm in explaining the bibli
in this book. Whether you've be
out of the world or you're happy .... where you are, *Chasing Contentment*
will refresh your perspective as you marvel at the sovereign joy of Jesus."
Gloria Furman, author, *Missional Motherhood* and *Alive in Him*

"Too often our search for contentment leads us to sources unable to bear the
weight of our desires. We trust in money, relationships, and circumstances,
only to find ourselves increasingly dissatisfied. This book helps to clarify
our understanding of contentment, as well as redirect our hopes to the One
who is able to provide lasting joy. Raymond combines wisdom from church
fathers with modern insights and examples that make this book readable,
applicable, and needed."
Melissa Kruger, Women's Ministry Coordinator, Uptown Church,
Charlotte, North Carolina; author, *The Envy of Eve*

"Just about every day, I wake up and read Erik Raymond's insights on pastoral ministry, discipleship, and everyday living as a Christian. He always
challenges me to love Jesus as I trust in the sufficiency of his work on the
cross. As someone who struggles with contentment, I need his wise counsel
to walk with Christ in freedom and joy."
Collin Hansen, Editorial Director, The Gospel Coalition; author,
Blind Spots

"In this book, my friend Erik Raymond isn't saying anything new—he's
reminding us of some very old wisdom that has gone unheeded and unher-
alded in our discontented age. Drawing from the prophets, the Puritans, and
his own personal experience, he puts his finger on our malaise and offers us
gospel medicine. I need the truth in this book—and I'm betting you do too."
Robert H. Thune, Lead Pastor, Coram Deo Church, Omaha, Nebraska

"Erik Raymond is the right man to write the book *Chasing Contentment*. I
was immensely blessed and challenged by this fine work. You will be too as
you read and apply it."
Jason Allen, President, Midwestern Baptist Theological Seminary
and College

"Does any word better define our culture than 'chasing'? Does any word better describe what's missing in our culture than 'contentment'? By pairing these seemingly contradictory words, Erik calls us to end our pursuit of more and to begin our pursuit of enough. Read this engaging and enjoyable exploration of Christian contentment and decide, as I did, that this chase is well worth the effort."

David Murray, Professor of Old Testament, Puritan Reformed Theological Seminary; Pastor, Grand Rapids Free Reformed Church, Grand Rapids, Michigan; author, *Jesus on Every Page* and *The Happy Christian*

"Erik Raymond is one of my favorite writers. Discontentment is one of my deepest struggles. What a joy, then, to have this author speak wisely, biblically, and pastorally about the value, the importance, and the pursuit of contentment. If you struggle as I do, you'll find help and hope in the pages of this book and, ultimately, in the Book of books it points to."

Tim Challies, blogger, Challies.com

"For decades, when asked for a book recommendation on Christian contentment, I always had to reference books by Puritans like Burroughs and Watson. I knew of no solid modern book on the matter—until now. Erik Raymond's *Chasing Contentment* is that modern work I have longed to see and use. This book contains the wisdom and insights of the timeless Puritan works, yet brings a culturally relevant pastoral sensitivity that will make this the go-to book on this subject—thoroughly biblical, immensely practical. I highly commend this book and the faithful man who wrote it."

Brian Croft, Senior Pastor, Auburndale Baptist Church; Founder, Practical Shepherding, Senior Fellow, Church Revitalization Center, The Southern Baptist Theological Seminary

Chasing Contentment

CHASING CONTENTMENT

TRUSTING GOD IN A DISCONTENTED AGE

Erik Raymond

WHEATON, ILLINOIS

Cover design: Jeff Miller, Faceout Studio

First printing 2017

Printed in the United States of America

Unless otherwise indicated, Scripture quotations are from the ESV® Bible (The Holy Bible, English Standard Version®), copyright © 2001 by Crossway, a publishing ministry of Good News Publishers. Used by permission. All rights reserved.

Scripture quotations marked NASB are from The New American Standard Bible®. Copyright © The Lockman Foundation 1960, 1962, 1963, 1968, 1971, 1972, 1973, 1975, 1977, 1995. Used by permission.

Trade paperback ISBN: 978-1-4335-5366-0
ePub ISBN: 978-1-4335-5369-1
PDF ISBN: 978-1-4335-5367-7
Mobipocket ISBN: 978-1-4335-5368-4

Library of Congress Cataloging-in-Publication Data

Names: Raymond, Erik, author.
Title: Chasing contentment: trusting God in a discontented age / Erik Raymond.
Description: Wheaton: Crossway, 2017. | Includes bibliographical references and index.
Identifiers: LCCN 2016030032 (print) | LCCN 2016036982 (ebook) | ISBN 9781433553660 (tp) | ISBN 9781433553677 (pdf) | ISBN 9781433553684 (mobi) | ISBN 9781433553691 (epub)
Subjects: LCSH: Contentment—Religious aspects—Christianity. | Trust in God (Christianity)
Classification: LCC BV4647.C7 R39 2017 (print) | LCC BV4647.C7 (ebook) | DDC 248.4—dc23
LC record available at https://lccn.loc.gov/2016030032

Crossway is a publishing ministry of Good News Publishers.

VP		27	26	25	24	23	22	21	20	19	18	17
15	14	13	12	11	10	9	8	7	6	5	4	3	2	1

To the Lord Jesus Christ,
who brings us back to God (1 Pet. 3:18)

Contents

Preface. 11

Introduction. 14

Part 1
DEFINING CONTENTMENT

1   Understanding Contentment. 21

2   The God Who Is Content. 34

Part 2
LEARNING CONTENTMENT

3   Better Than I Deserve. 51

4   Left, Right, Left 64

5   See Through the Shiny Wrappers. 81

6   Just Say No! 97

7   Be Still and Know 112

8   Be a Faithful Bride 129

9   You Are Not Yet Home. 146

Conclusion. 162

General Index. 167

Scripture Index. 171

Preface

There's a story behind every book. The story behind this book is painfully sweet. A couple of years ago I was enduring a particularly difficult season. It seemed as though God had allowed affliction to hover like a rain cloud over my life. Pastoral ministry was especially trying even as I encountered a number of new health problems. This, along with the regular stiff headwind of living in a fallen world, had me weary.

But I was more than weary. I was restless. And, upon further review, I was discontent. In God's providence I was preaching through the book of Hebrews at the time. The thick, dark rain clouds of affliction cast a shadow over my studies and even, I regret, some of my preaching. Looking back, I am reminded of William Cowper's hymn "God Moves in a Mysterious Way." He writes:

> Ye fearful saints, fresh courage take!
> The clouds ye so much dread
> Are big with mercy and shall break
> In blessings on your head.
>
> Judge not the Lord by feeble sense,
> But trust him for his grace;
> Behind a frowning providence
> He hides a smiling face.[1]

---

1. William Cowper, "God Moves in a Mysterious Way," 1774.

One day as I opened my Bible to study, the clouds burst with blessings on my head. I read in chapter 13 of Hebrews:

> Be content with what you have, for he has said, "I will never leave you nor forsake you." So we can confidently say,
>
> > "The Lord is my helper;
> > I will not fear;
> > what can man do to me?" (Heb. 13:5–6)

Through these verses God began to remind me afresh that despite anything, I can (and must) be content in God. He is the source of my contentment, not my circumstances. Furthermore, my contentment will be fed by God's Word.

This led to me scribbling down questions, thoughts, confessions, and fresh discoveries of grace. Over the next several weeks, I marinated in this text and the subject of contentment. I preached, wrote, and talked with members of our congregation. God was teaching us about contentment. He was teaching us about who he is and how our contentment ultimately is in him. Indeed, behind a frowning providence he hides a smiling face. Seeing this face, through the eyes of faith, serves to create and sustain contentment.

This book explains what contentment is and several ways to learn it. It is pivotal to understand that contentment is anchored in the God who is content in himself. What better gift can God give to hungry, hurting people like us than himself? He welcomes us to his banquet hall to find our souls satisfied in him. Contentment is the abiding "Amen" of our joy. But we need to know more than what contentment is; we need to know how to learn it and practice it. In Philippians 4:11, Paul remarks that he learned how to be content. How then do we learn this? In the second part of this book I lay out some practical ways we can learn to be content.

I am thankful that over the course of time in writing this book God answered prayers to help make me content in him. As you might expect, he did this by means of various trials. I had the privilege of applying what I was writing to my life in real time. I also applied what I was living to what I was writing. In other words, we don't graduate from the school of contentment; we're career students. Whether you are writing or reading a book on the subject, God will faithfully and graciously provide areas where you can learn contentment. It's in this sense that we are all continually chasing contentment even while we know something about it and what its footprints look like in our lives. I pray that this book will further your study at the school of contentment.

— — —

I am grateful for so many helping hands in this project. Thank you, everyone at Crossway, for your joyful service in publishing books that serve the church. In particular, thank you, Justin Taylor, Dave DeWit, Thom Notaro, Amy Kruis, Lauren Harvey, and Josh Dennis.

Thank you to my former boss and pastor, Pat Abendroth, for encouraging me early on to consider writing. It seemed strange at the time, but in God's providence you have blessed me deeply by shepherding me in that direction, brother. Thank you, Emmaus Bible Church, the church where I am privileged to serve as pastor. Your prayers, feedback, and encouragement served me more than you will know.

Thank you to Matt Fudge, a dear friend and fellow elder, for your thoughtful conversations about the Trinity and contentment. Thank you, Luke Gorsett, for so many helpful discussions about this subject while working out at the gym.

Thank you to my children—Bryce, Luke, Alaynah, Alexis, Zoë, and Bo; you are such a bouquet of grace to me. And my loving wife, Christie, thank you for your persistent reminders to keep seeking the things above, where Christ is (Col. 3:1–4), and for your encouragement to write this book in the first place. You are truly an excellent wife, my best friend, and my dear sister. What a privilege it is to walk to Immanuel's land while holding your hand.

Introduction

If you drive through rural New England towns, you'll notice an abundance of stone walls. These walls initially served as property markers hundreds of years ago; and because they were well built, many remain to this day. But the art of building stone walls has nearly faded away. The craftsmen who make them, though plentiful in a previous age, are now few.

Some years ago my dad (who lives in New England) wanted to have a wall built on his property that reflected some of this old-world craftsmanship. As he inquired as to who could do it, he found the list of prospects to be remarkably small. When the selected mason came, it was like he had just stepped out of a time machine. His tools, his work ethic, and even the way he spoke about the wall seemed to be from another time. He represented something of the lost art of masonry.

I wonder if you've experienced something like this when you've read Christian biographies or older theological works. They reflect a level of depth and devotion that seems uncommon today. I've run into this when I've read some of the Puritan writers. One topic they talk about regularly and thoroughly is contentment. Reading their sermons and books, I sometimes feel like I am hearing voices from another world.

Is contentment a lost art? Is it simply a product of yesterday's Christianity? Are there only a few "craftsmen" left who practice it? And if so, is this okay with God?

I don't think it is. In fact, I'm certain it's not. Hebrews 13:5 commands us, "Be content with what you have." And the apostle Paul demonstrates his own personal contentment in his letter to the Philippian church: "Not that I am speaking of being in need, for I have learned in whatever situation I am to be content. I know how to be brought low, and I know how to abound. In any and every circumstance, I have learned the secret of facing plenty and hunger, abundance and need" (Phil. 4:11–12). We should remember that the writer of Hebrews was addressing a church when he gave his command, and Paul was likewise writing to a local church when he discussed his priority and practice of contentment. In other words, contentment is for the church, and that includes us today. Instead of being something from a bygone age, contentment is to be a priority for all Christians.

You may find yourself convicted and perhaps even discouraged by thinking about contentment. Let me encourage you not to stay there. Did you happen to see that hopeful phrase in Philippians 4:12, "I have learned"? The apostle Paul himself had to learn contentment. It was no more natural for him than it is for you. Learning contentment is a process for all believers. Furthermore, it should encourage you that he did in fact learn it. In other words, it is attainable. He could look at his life, while in prison, and say that he learned the art of being content. In any and every situation, he knew that he had found the secret of contentment. While you may feel discouraged when you sense your discontentment, you should be encouraged to see that contentment is something attainable. Even more than this, contentment is something that God commands and provides the grace to experience.

In this book I want to help you to pursue contentment. I am not writing as someone who has been particularly successful at it. Like many other Christians, I have seasons when I feel like I am doing better than at other times. I continue to learn just like everyone else. In fact, it was a season in life a couple of years ago that God especially used to teach me how to be content in him.

At the time, I was preaching through Hebrews. When I reached chapter 13, I was captivated by what I found:

> Keep your life free from love of money, and be content with what you have, for he has said, "I will never leave you nor forsake you." So we can confidently say,
>
> > "The Lord is my helper;
> > I will not fear;
> > what can man do to me?" (Heb. 13:5–6)

Here the writer commands believers to be content, reminds them of God's providence, restates God's promises, and looks ahead to the end of the age. And all this is found in a book that gloriously exalts the supremacy and sufficiency of Christ. Add to this my own personal burden and struggles with contentment at the time, and you have some well-tilled soil ready for the divine gardener to work. And he did work. I studied, read, prayed, talked, and preached. I went into a contentment bubble for weeks. Much of what I taught in our church found its way into this book. The entire process was helpful to me. But even while looking back, I can see that I'm still learning to be content along with the rest of our congregation.

While studying this topic, I found a couple of friends to be very helpful. Think of them as craftsmen from the old world. The first was the English Puritan Jeremiah Burroughs (1599–1646). A pastor and author, Burroughs wrote the classic *The Rare Jewel of Christian Contentment.*[1] The second was Thomas Watson (1620–1686), also an English Puritan, pastor, and author. His book *The Art of Divine Contentment*[2] is an apologetic for biblical contentment. Often striking the same chords as Burroughs, Watson layers his teaching in word pictures and imagery to make the case that

---

1. Jeremiah Burroughs, *The Rare Jewel of Christian Contentment* (Edinburgh: Banner of Truth, 1979).
2. Thomas Watson, *The Art of Divine Contentment: An Exposition of Philippians 4:11,* accessed April 1, 2016, http://www.biblebb.com/files/TW/tw-contentment.htm.

we as Christians must pursue contentment in Christ. Both Burroughs and Watson faced adversity in ministry, including poverty, rejection, and (in the case of Watson) imprisonment. These were tough times for both men, but through such adversity their writings were forged. Their hearts and souls are in their books. And through their pens the enduring testimony of God's sufficiency extends to our day as well.

Throughout this book I will rely on both authors. Often I will quote them, interact with them, and update their language. But their imprint extends beyond quotations, and much of what I write here is born of lengthy time reading and contemplating what they wrote. I am grateful to God for their inescapable influence.

It is my prayer that as you read this book and consider the topic of contentment, you will find yourself drawn to God as the source and sustainer of your contentment.

Review Questions

1. Before reading this introduction, did you think of contentment as something that was realistic or idealistic? Why?

2. Does the prospect of learning contentment appeal to you? Or does it unsettle you? Explain.

3. In the past, how has the example of godly saints from church history influenced your Christian life?

Part 1

DEFINING CONTENTMENT

1

Understanding Contentment

Tom Brady is one of my favorite athletes of all time. He is an ardent competitor, a practical joker, and a flat-out sensational quarterback for my hometown team. One of the things I appreciate about Brady is his candor. In a 2005 interview with *60 Minutes* the quarterback said:

> Why do I have three Super Bowl rings and still think there's something greater out there for me? I mean, maybe a lot of people would say, "Hey man, this is what is [important]." I reached my goal, my dream, my life. Me, I think, "God, it's got to be more than this." I means this isn't, this can't be what it's all cracked up to be.[1]

Brady is absolutely not satisfied. Prior to the 2015 season and coming off of a 2014 Super Bowl championship (his fourth), he released a video[2] in which he said, "You know what my favorite ring is? The next one." Let's remember that he says these things

1. Daniel Schorn, "Tom Brady: The Winner," *CBSNews*, November 3, 2005, updated December 20, 2007, http://www.cbsnews.com/news/tom-brady-the-winner.
2. "Tom Brady, Patriots on to 'The Next One' in QB'S Facebook Hype Video," *NESN*, September 10, 2015, http://nesn.com/2015/09/tom-brady-patriots-on-to-the-next-one-in -pump-up-facebook-video.

from the top of a social mountaintop. From an achievement stand-point, he has it all. He has plenty of money, fame, success, and respect from his peers. He is married to a supermodel, has healthy and happy children, and lives in a mansion. But when you listen to him, he sounds like a guy who just watched an overhyped movie. He's never satisfied.

Some might interpret his words as showing how driven he is. I'm sure that's part of it. But there's more. He is restlessly search-ing. He is scratching his head with his hand adorned with four championship rings and asking, Is there more than this?

Many of Tom Brady's experiences are unique to an All-Pro NFL quarterback, but discontentment is common to us all. We relativize and minimize our impatience. We laugh and joke about big splurge purchases that "we just had to have." Complaining is second nature for us. Instead of running to the Lord in prayer or being content to be wronged, we often grumble and complain.

Have you ever noticed that people say they're very busy, yet ev-erywhere they go they're on their phones scrolling through social media? When you post something online, have you noticed how many people ask you about it? Often these are the same people who are so busy!

Some cultural observers have noted a growing phenomenon called fear of missing out (FOMO). With so much information at our fingertips we become restless wondering what our friends are doing, whether we have any emails, what is happening in politics— anything other than what we are doing at the moment. FOMO may explain our constant connectedness, but discontentment explains FOMO. Discontent comes because we are restless, unhappy, unsat-isfied, and curious. It seems that within a few decades of technologi-cal development, many can scarcely engage in the menial tasks of life for very long without checking their phones. It's as if we're say-ing, "I have learned in whatever situation I am in to be discontent."

Contrast this with the words of the apostle Paul in Philippians 4:11: "I have learned in whatever situation I am to be content."

The cry of the hearts of all people, whether rich or poor, is for more. They are discontent. The heartbeat of Paul in this text is that whether he has a lot or not very much, he has what he needs. He is content. We all naturally fall into the first group. We thirst for and pursue more. But as Christians we are called to live in the company of the apostle, to say we've tasted and are satisfied—we have what we need. We are to be after the elusive but ever-prized jewel of contentment.

Before going further, we need a clear definition of contentment. After all, we want to know where we are going and when we arrive there. So, what exactly is contentment? Leaning heavily upon others,[3] I offer this definition: contentment is the inward, gracious, quiet spirit that joyfully rests in God's providence.

Have you been to an orchestral performance and witnessed the tuning process? It almost seems like part of the performance itself as the musicians allow each other to go ahead and tune their instruments prior to beginning. As I sit in the audience, I am fascinated by the carefulness and patience exhibited by the musicians to ensure that they are on the same page. This is what this chapter aims to do. It is a "sync up" or tuning, if you will, to a biblical understanding of contentment. As we walk through the definition, we will certainly identify some areas that are out of tune. That's okay. The goal is to build the foundation and then learn this art of contentment.

Contentment Comes from the Inside Out

Think with me about Paul and Silas sitting in a Philippian jail. The authorities had ordered them to be bound in the "inner prison" or dungeon, as we might say. Their feet were fastened in the stocks. These were the same stocks often used to torture prisoners in the ancient world. But to get an accurate picture we must remember how Paul and Silas got there.

---

3. Especially Jeremiah Burroughs, *The Rare Jewel of Christian Contentment* (Edinburgh: Banner of Truth, 1979).

The book of Acts tells us that earlier in the day, they were preaching the gospel in the town of Philippi and seeing fruit. In fact, the impact of their preaching was such that the local industry of fortune-tellers feared for their business. Feeling desperate, they attacked Paul and Silas and dragged them into court. Soon a mob of people began physically attacking them, and the rulers tore the evangelists' clothes, stripped them naked, and ordered that they be beaten with rods. After Paul and Silas had been sufficiently beaten, the magistrates ordered that they be thrown into the dungeon and locked in the stocks (Acts 16:19–24).

By all accounts this was a rough day. If there was ever a day when we would expect Paul to complain or at least grumble a bit, this was it. But we don't see that at all. In fact, we see quite the opposite. "About midnight Paul and Silas were praying and singing hymns to God, and the prisoners were listening to them" (Acts 16:25).

What we read in verse 25 is astounding in light of what we read in verse 24. Paul and Silas, after being stripped and publicly beaten with rods, were hauled off to prison and thrown into the dark, musty basement where they were fastened in the stocks. If this were a movie, the camera would zoom in on the missionaries and then fade out. They would look pitiable. These are horrible circumstances. The film would let us know that a few hours have passed when guards come in to check on the poor, beleaguered evangelists. Expecting to find them either dead or groaning, we'd discover them praying and singing hymns to God!

These guys not only had enough strength to live, but they had the will, the desire to sing and pray to God. When we read of them together like this, we can almost see the narrator's smile as he includes this nugget: "and the prisoners were listening to them" (Acts 16:24). I bet they were.

Here's the million-dollar question: How could people who had been through what they'd been through and then endured the circumstances they were enduring find it in themselves to lead a prayer meeting and a hymn sing? Here's the simple answer: they were content. Paul says as much in a letter to the church he planted in this same town, "Not that I am speaking of being in need, for I have learned in whatever situation I am to be content. I know how to be brought low, and I know how to abound. In any and every circumstance, I have learned the secret of facing plenty and hunger, abundance and need" (Phil. 4:11–12).

Contentment is not based upon circumstances. It can't be. Paul and Silas were content in some of the worst circumstances imaginable. Their singing in the midst of terrible circumstances shows that contentment works inside out. But doesn't this seem counterintuitive? So often we think that if we could just change our circumstances, we could be happy. We are restless because of what we perceive as difficult circumstances. We focus our attention on our jobs, health, relationships, children's behavior, problems at church, physical appearance, and so on. "If this would just change, then my life would be so much better."

This is where we see that contentment is far more powerful than a change of circumstances. Instead of being sourced on the outside and subject to changing circumstances, biblical contentment comes from within and endures through the spectrum of circumstances. How else can we explain the singing that filled the Philippian dungeon?

This is part of the tuning process that we need to undergo. If at the very outset we misunderstand contentment, then we can't possibly come to fully enjoy its immense blessing. On the other hand, if we realize that at its heart contentment is not primarily about what's outside us but about what's inside of us, we will be well on our way toward learning this lost art.

Contentment Is Quiet

Just as we can learn a lot about people by listening to them talk, we can learn a lot about ourselves by doing the same thing. When you talk about other people, are you generally charitable or complaining? When you discuss your job or church, are you prone to grumble or to emphasize what is good? If you are comfortable enough to cut through the fog of superficial politeness with people and answer the question "How are you doing?" do you tend to be negative? Jesus taught us that what we say comes from our heart (Matt. 12:34). What is in the well comes up in the bucket. If your heart were a body of water, would it be a peaceful lake or a stormy sea? A contented heart showcases itself by not grumbling or complaining (Phil. 2:14).

I should nuance this a bit, because there is a type of biblical complaining that is healthy. I am not saying that we should be numb or insensitive to the difficulties of life. Contentment does not mean ignoring problems or pretending they don't exist. Quite the opposite! A contented spirit is one that realizes the difficulty but can nevertheless rest in God in the midst of it.

Second, contentment does not mean that we don't voice our complaints to God. The Scriptures are full of prayers from godly people who cry out and complain to God (e.g., Pss. 3:4; 34:6; 55:16–17; 77:1; 142:1–3). In fact, we are commanded to cast our cares upon the Lord (1 Pet. 5:7). The motive for this is that he cares for us. But mark the contrast; there is a difference between complaining to God ("How long, O LORD?") and complaining about God. The first is supported by an enduring trust that God hears and loves. The second is betrayed by an eroding trust that God hears and loves. It is a privilege for Christians to bring their burdened hearts to their Father for soul medicine.

Finally, contentment is not opposed to seeking help from others for deliverance out of present afflictions by lawful means. Jeremiah Burroughs makes this point clearly when he shows that contentment is not at odds with using God's means to find relief from affliction: "And so far as he leads me I may follow his providence." We seek help in such a way that we are submissive to God's will and how God wills. In this, says Burroughs, "our wills are melted into the will of God. This is not opposed to the quietness which God requires in a contented spirit."[4]

The complaining of discontentment includes grumbling. The grumbling is a distrust of God, an anxious concern that the future won't work out the way we want it to. Discontentment can also be characterized by bitterness. This is a frustration that the past has not gone the way we'd like. Further, discontentment can be characterized by distraction in the present. Unable to focus on what should be prized and prioritized today, the discontented heart rages amid its busyness and worldliness (1 John 2:16–17). Whether explicitly or implicitly, this type of grumbling is directed at the One who is sovereign over such things. Grumbling and complaining, then, are a theological issue that casts God as incompetent, unfair, or irrelevant. We can see why discontentment is considered unchristian.

It may be helpful, when thinking about contentment, to ask those close to you if they think you often complain. Consider what you talk about. Inventory what you think about. Are you consistently embracing God's goodness in the valleys as well as on the mountaintops? Contentment knows how to sing in the stocks as well as at the banquet feast.

Contentment Is a Work of Grace

Earlier we saw that contentment works from the inside out. Now I want to push that a bit further along. The inward working of God upon the heart is the work of grace. How else can we explain such strange behavior?

If we are honest, at first blush this discourages us. "You mean I can't do this? I can't gin up the effort to get it done?" It's true—you can't. In fact, if you try to, you will fail miserably and even fuel further discontentment. But as we begin to think about this inability, it's actually quite encouraging. The fact that Paul (and

---

4. Ibid., 22.

so many others) lived with contentment can give us hope. In other words, God has a track record of making people like you and me content in him. As we will see in the next chapter in more detail, one of the functions of the gospel is to fix our hearts upon God. We move from restless to resting, from hurting to healed, and from hungry to satisfied. God makes otherwise restless people content in him (Ps. 73:26). This is a work of grace.

When the Philippian Christians first got the apostle Paul's letter, they would have recognized Paul's call to contentment as revolutionary. In their culture, contentment was a key topic of ethical discussion from the time of Socrates.

> In Stoic philosophy it [contentment] denotes the one who "becomes an independent man sufficient to himself and in need of none else." The goal for the Stoic was that "a man should be sufficient unto himself for all things, and able, by the power of his own will, to resist the force of circumstances." . . . By the exercise of reason over emotions, the Stoic learns to be content. For the Stoic, emotional detachment is essential in order to be content.[5]

What a stark difference for the Christian. Instead of achieving contentment through being strong in reason, the Christian learns contentment by being weak enough to be strengthened by grace.

At this point you might be saying, "I'm not much of a complainer; I'm involved in my church, and I think overall I'm fairly content." The challenge is to look honestly at the evidence in our lives. Can we be sure we've learned contentment by grace? Has this worked inside out? Or are we simply consoled by having the things we want? This is an important question.

---

5. G. Walter Hansen, *The Letter to the Philippians* (Grand Rapids, MI: Eerdmans, 2009), 310; Hansen quotes Gerhard Kittel, "αὐτάρκεια, αὐτάρκης," in *Theological Dictionary of the New Testament*, ed. Gerhard Kittel and Gerhard Friedrich, trans. Geoffrey W. Bromiley, 10 vols. (Grand Rapids, MI: Eerdmans, 1964–1976), 1:466, and Marvin R. Vincent, *A Critical and Exegetical Commentary on the Epistles to the Philippians and to Philemon* (New York: Scribner's, 1897), 143n11; he also cites Abraham J. Malherbe, "Paul's Self-Sufficiency," in *Friendship, Flattery, and Frankness of Speech*, ed. John T. Fitzgerald (Leiden: Brill, 1996), 126, and G. W. Peterman, *Paul's Gift from Philippi* (New York: Cambridge University Press, 1997), 136.

Think about a crying baby who finds consolation when given a toy. Is she content from the inside out? Of course not. Take away the toy and you'll discover soon enough the source of her contentment! The same is true for grown men and women. We have a smile and a peace when work is going well, the bills are being paid, and the kids are minding. But what happens when something goes awry? Has this contentment been worked inside out by means of grace? Or is this happiness similar to a baby's with a toy? The source of our quietness is revealed by how we respond when God brings a trial.

Contentment Joyfully Rests in God's Providence

Embracing the doctrine of providence is vital for learning the art of contentment. In chapter 7 we will look into this further, but for now we should at least set the table a bit. Providence teaches us that God is not disconnected from what is happening in the world today. There is no such thing as chance, luck, or fate. Rather, an all-wise, loving, powerful God is upholding, governing, and ordering all things as if they come from his very hand. The Heidelberg Catechism says it very well in its section for Lord's Day 10:

> God's providence is his almighty and ever present power, whereby, as with his hand, he still upholds heaven and earth and all creatures, and so governs them that leaf and blade, rain and drought, fruitful and barren years, food and drink, health and sickness, riches and poverty, indeed, all things, come to us not by chance but by his fatherly hand.

A biblical example of where this doctrine reveals contentment is the story of Joseph. He was one of the twelve sons of Jacob. Joseph's older brothers became jealous of him because of their father's favored treatment of him. Jacob had made him a special coat that Joseph no doubt proudly wore before his brothers. What's more, Joseph had a dream in which his brothers were all bowing down before him. And to make matters worse, he told his brothers about the dream. This led to their plotting to kill him. When cooler heads prevailed, they decided instead to sell him into slavery and tell their father that Joseph was tragically killed by an animal.

After all of this plotting, Joseph ended up in Egypt, where he was promoted through the ranks and became the lead guy for Potiphar. Things were looking up for Joseph until the king's wife falsely accused Joseph of attempted rape after her failed efforts to seduce him. As a result, he was thrown into prison. While there, he interpreted dreams for some other prisoners and made a name for having wisdom. Later, Pharaoh called on him for this same purpose. Joseph shined in the moment and was given great honor in Egypt.

Meanwhile there was a famine in the land, and Joseph's brothers all felt its impact. So they made their way down to Egypt to ask for food. Through a series of events Joseph, while keeping his identity veiled to his brothers, provided for them and persuaded them all to come to Egypt. At last he revealed his true identity to his brothers, and they were gripped with fear of his revenge. But Joseph spoke something profound in reply: "As for you, you meant evil against me, but God meant it for good, to bring it about that many people should be kept alive, as they are today" (Gen. 50:20).

Do you see the chord of the doctrine of providence empowering this verse? God used all of the trouble that Joseph endured, even the malevolence of his brothers, for God's glory and the people's good. Joseph was strengthened by this truth from the inside out.

Now, think back to the baby playing with the toy or the adult with the good job. What if God were to take away what currently makes you happy, like he took away Joseph's fancy coat and seat of honor? What if providence brought you to a pit?

One thing is for sure; it would reveal whether your contentment were an inward work of grace or an external consoling by created things. Burroughs shows this contrast with an illustration. He says that to be content as a result of something external is like warming a man's clothes by the fire. But to be content through an inward work of grace in the soul is like the warmth that a man's clothes have from the natural heat of the body. If he is in good health, he puts on his clothes and perhaps at first on a cold morning they feel cold, but after a little while they are warm. How do they get warm? They haven't been next to the fire or on the heater. Instead, the warmth comes from the natural heat of the man's body. On the other hand, when a man is sick, he often has difficulty staying warm as his natural body heat has deteriorated. When this man puts on his clothes, they won't get warm. He has to go and sit by the fire or next to the heater to get warm. Even so, after a little while they will again be cold.

This illustrates our spiritual health. Suppose someone loses his job or gets some very difficult medical news; his first reaction is probably going to be shock. His spirit will feel the chill of the matter, like the chill of cold clothes. But after a time, the healthy believer who is fueled by grace will begin to make the affliction more bearable. Grace will heat him up, so to speak. On the other hand, to someone who does not have the inward glow of the gospel, such news is cold not only initially but continually. Friends may help him reason through it and surround him with loving support, but like the heat from the fire, this warmth will soon fade. Only what comes from a gracious spirit will endure.

I remember when an older brother in the church tactfully pointed out to me the need and practicality of resting in God's providence. Early in our marriage, Christie and I bought our first home. It was in a sketchy part of town, but it was all we could afford and we made it work. Over the years we saw a lot of things that made us say, "We should really move." After having our first daughter—our third child—we prayerfully pursued a move. Our house sold in three days, and we quickly found a home in another neighborhood that had fewer police helicopters overhead.

Upon moving in we had an open house, and dozens of friends came over. Amid the celebration I was on my deck with this same brother in Christ, who was about fifteen years my senior. There I stood smiling and reveling in God's goodness under the dark sky and bright decorative outside lights. My friend smiled wryly and surprised me by asking, "And he would still be good if he took it all away, right?" I almost dropped my drink. My startled look mimicked a Labrador upon hearing a dog whistle. "Yes he would," I replied slowly, yet I remember thinking, *What's with this guy? What a wet blanket!* But he wasn't a wet blanket at all. He was a man who had walked through affliction and had come out trusting. Perhaps he sensed that I was sounding a bit too much like a baby with a rattle instead of a Christian content in God. He made his point that night, and more than a dozen years later he is still making his point to me.

— — —

The danger of an oft-neglected word like *contentment* is that we may not have a firm grasp on what it actually means. If we are going to learn the art of contentment, then we'll need to know what it is and what it is not. Here, early in our journey, we have considered that contentment is inward as opposed to external. It is quiet rather than complaining. It is a work of grace rather than a result of human effort. It rests in God's providence rather than complaining against him. With this we have the instruments of our minds tuned by grace.

Review Questions

1. What does the testimony of rich, successful celebrities teach us about the elusive nature of contentment?

2. How could Paul and Silas sing and pray while in such a miserable place as a first-century Roman dungeon?

3. Why is it important to understand that contentment is not based on circumstances?

4. From what you've read in this chapter, do you think that your heart is quiet (resting) or noisy (complaining)?

5. Consider again Burroughs's illustration of warming one's clothes by the fire versus by the health and heat of the body. Identify experiences where the work of God's grace has warmed your soul amid the cold temperature of affliction.

2

The God Who Is Content

Soon after I was converted, I noticed that Christians often talked in what seemed like a foreign language. They tossed words around that I'd never heard before and leaned on concepts that were entirely unfamiliar to me. Having not grown up in a Christian home, I felt a bit lost, even though I had recently been found. So I asked a lot of questions, but mostly I asked why. Gracious brothers and sisters would smile and patiently answer my questions. I am so grateful for the many people who endured my questions with grace and love.

More than fifteen years later I'm still asking why. When we come to a topic like contentment, it seems like people generally know the answers to the questions. If we were to walk into ten Bible-believing churches and ask, "Are Christians supposed to be content?" most people would probably say yes. But what would they say if we asked them why? Some might say they don't know, but others would probably say that the Bible says so.

Why should I be content in God? And how do I do it? What's the big deal if I don't? What is competing with my contentment? And why is it competing with it? You see, there is a lot more to the why question than simple church-speak. God is a big God. Not only can he answer our questions, but he delights to.

We need to think biblically and carefully about this topic. When we do, we quickly realize that contentment is something we greatly desire but find elusive. This struggle is not unique to a few restless souls; it is common to us all. However, we are not without a framework for it. In fact, our universal restlessness and pursuit of a soul-steadying experience reveals a fascinating insight into our humanity: we were created to be content. C. S. Lewis astutely observed that the presence of an unsatisfied, unabated longing would seem to indicate that we were created to be satisfied by something from another world.[1] In other words, the world and how we experience it cannot bring the bubble into the center of the level. Left to our natural inclinations and patterns, we will always be restlessly off-center.

The key to experiencing contentment is learning where it comes from, why it is elusive, and how to get it.

Where Does Contentment Come From?

Imagine traveling back to the very beginning of time. Just to the left of the words "in the beginning" in Genesis 1:1, there is no creation yet—no earth and no people, animals, plants, or oceans to fill it. We see nothing. But that does not mean that nothing exists. We know from the Bible—even from the earliest words in Genesis—that God existed prior to creation and brought it about by his sovereign will (Gen. 1:1). But what was God doing? Where was he? What was he like? Was he bored? Lonely? Insecure?

Consider the Source

Before we can answer these questions, there's a more fundamental question: who is God? The Bible teaches us that God is one. That is, he is one in his essence or being. At the same time, God exists in three distinct, coequal, and coeternal persons who glorify and enjoy one another. These three persons are the Father, the Son, and

---

1. C. S. Lewis, *Mere Christianity* (New York: HarperSanFrancisco, 2009), 26.

the Holy Spirit. We call this one God in three persons the Trinity. When we peer over the fence prior to Genesis 1:1, we find ourselves looking in on one God who exists in the beautifully diverse and unified community of the Trinity. We are looking into what Fred Sanders calls "the happy land of the Trinity."[2]

Who do we see when we look over this fence? The Scriptures tell us much about God that helps to inform and shape our understanding of him.

God is eternal. This simply means that God has no beginning and no end. He is not bound by time but "sees events in time and acts in time"[3] (see Ps. 90:2).

God is unchanging. God has never changed, nor will he ever change. We will never see a fourth member of the Trinity added, nor will God ever cease to be. He is and forever will be the eternal "I am" (Ps. 102:26; Mal. 3:6; John 8:58).

God is independent. God does not need anything or anyone. He is self-sufficient. As Louis Berkhof states, "God has the ground of his existence in himself and, unlike man, does not depend on anything outside of himself. He is independent in his being, in his virtues, and actions, and independence causes all his creatures to depend on him. The idea is embodied in the name Jehovah"[4] (Acts 17:25; Rev. 4:11).

God is love. At its heart, love is about giving rather than taking. God's self-giving love is so essential to his character that John declares, "God is love" (1 John 4:8). We often think of God's love expressed to his creation (and rightly so), but we should not overlook God's love *prior to* creation. In his High Priestly Prayer, Jesus cited the love he had with his Father before the foundation of the world (John 17:24). He also disclosed that a reason for his

---

2. Fred Sanders, *The Deep Things of God: How the Trinity Changes Everything* (Wheaton, IL: Crossway, 2010), 61.
3. Wayne A. Grudem, *Systematic Theology: An Introduction to Biblical Doctrine* (Leicester: Inter-Varsity Press, 1994), 168.
4. Louis Berkhof, *A Summary of Christian Doctrine* (London: Banner of Truth, 1960), 24.

obedience to the Father's will was that the world would know that he, the Son, loves the Father (John 14:31).

God is committed to his glory. Because God is God, he is committed to having his glory (worth, renown, fame, or value) seen and savored.[5] This means that everything God does is with the goal of communicating his glory. That includes intra-Trinitarian and extra-Trinitarian communication—expressions of God's glory within the eternal Trinity and the revelation of his glory throughout history. God pursues and promotes his infinite worth and beauty in every instance (Isa. 42:8).

When we put this together, we see that God has neither beginning nor end and is unchanging, self-sufficient, overflowing in self-giving love, and unflinchingly committed to his own glory. To put it another way, we could say that God is and has forever been perfectly content in himself.

Have you ever thought of God as being content? It is pivotal for us, as we strive to learn contentment, that we see God in this light. The Bible portrays him as both the object and the model of contentment. He is content in himself, and he shows us that the only way to find contentment is in him. Therefore, as we peer over the fence into the mysteriously "happy land of the Trinity," we see the God who is perfectly content in himself.

Creation as an Overflow and Not a Deficit

The understanding that God is content helps us to have a biblical framework for the doctrine of creation. Often people talk about God the Creator as if he were sitting around twiddling his thumbs, consumed by boredom or loneliness. How different is this from what we have seen in the Scriptures? Fred Sanders gets it exactly right when he observes, "God did not create the world in order to fill the drafty mansion of heaven with the pitter-patter of little feet. God is not pining away for companionship in a lonesome

---

5. This helpful tandem of verbs comes from John Piper, *Seeing and Savoring Jesus Christ* (Wheaton, IL: Crossway, 2001).

heaven."[6] When God created, he did so not out of lack but out of abundance. It was the overflow of Trinitarian love and a commitment to his glory that compelled God to create. The entire universe is a divinely constructed amphitheater to host the ongoing proclamation of God's glory.

> The heavens declare the glory of God,
>   and the sky above proclaims his handiwork.
> Day to day pours out speech,
>   and night to night reveals knowledge. (Ps. 19:1–2)

Any attempt to understand contentment must begin with God. As the only uncreated being, he is the only one who is not dependent on someone or something else. He is entirely self-sufficient. And as such, he alone is eligible to be the source of any true and lasting contentment. This is pretty straightforward. But why is contentment so elusive?

Why Is Contentment So Elusive?

We as people are often stuck in the mud of the messiness of life. And if we are not presently in the throes of a major life event, we are most certainly restless from the persistent gnats of life that irritate and unsettle us. Because of this, encountering someone like the apostle Paul in his letter to the Philippians is like running into a unicorn on your evening walk. It is like a story we might wish to believe, but our deflated experience overrules our imaginations.

We know from the Bible that God gave humanity the distinct privilege of being crowned the pinnacle of creation. As people, we alone were given the honor of being made in God's image (Gen. 1:26–28). God has stamped his image or likeness upon us so that we would reflect and represent him in the world he has created. The way we will properly reflect and represent God is by obey-

---

6. Sanders, *The Deep Things of God*, 95.

ing his Word. God's Word lovingly tells us what's right and what's wrong. It tells us what is true, good, and beautiful. Through the Word of God we are given a clear path for our walk. In other words, we fulfill our purpose as people through God-glorifying obedience to his Word.

Rules have fallen on hard times. Questioning authority has become a virtue, and resisting authority a social badge. Teenagers feel this when they begin to bristle at the authority of their parents. But, of course, rules are meant not to harm or deprive us but to keep us safe. Recently a woman in Omaha decided she didn't approve of the rules that restricted her access to the zoo.[7] After a night of drinking, she broke into the zoo and crossed several lines. As you might imagine, she ended up getting an unpleasant welcome—from a tiger—and suffered injuries. The rules were meant to help her, not hurt her. Though rules are restrictive, that does not mean they are bad or contrary to our good.

Why exactly does God give us instruction? Why does he issue commands? Certainly there is an element of informing, even warning, involved. But fundamentally there is more. Early in Genesis, God speaks to Adam because he loves him. God's words are intended to instruct him in the way he should go so that he will continue resting and rejoicing in God. They are, therefore, words of love intended to secure joy, not words of malice plotting for Adam's ruin. Consider Genesis 1:28–31, where Adam is given dominion over all of creation:

> And God blessed them. And God said to them, "Be fruitful and multiply and fill the earth and subdue it, and have dominion over the fish of the sea and over the birds of the heavens and over every living thing that moves on the earth." And God said, "Behold, I have given you every plant yielding seed that is on the face of all the earth, and every tree with seed in

---

7. "Woman Sneaks into Henry Doorly Zoo, Is Bitten by Tiger," *KETV*, November 2, 2016, http://www.ketv.com/news/woman-sneaks-into-henry-doorly-zoo-is-bitten-by-tiger /36192512.

its fruit. You shall have them for food. And to every beast of the earth and to every bird of the heavens and to everything that creeps on the earth, everything that has the breath of life, I have given every green plant for food." And it was so. And God saw everything that he had made, and behold, it was very good. And there was evening and there was morning, the sixth day. (Gen. 1:28–31)

The text reads like a narrative of Christmas morning, as present after present is opened without any drop-off in quality. Everything meets God's standard for goodness, and God lovingly gives it to Adam to steward. After receiving the tour of the newly minted creation, including its pristine rivers and perfect garden, Adam is given a firm warning not to eat from a particular tree. The warning is accompanied by the sure consequence of death if unheeded (Gen. 2:17). At its simplest, the command from God is essentially saying: "If you try to make yourself happy by disobeying my words, you will become very, very unhappy. Instead of finding life, you will find death."

It is important to remember why God spoke to our first parents in the garden. He spoke to light their path. His word both warns about walking away and (later) shows the way back home. The warning about the tree serves to test whether they will find their contentment in God or will pursue it in created things.

We know the bad news of chapter 3. The Serpent's hiss aims to undermine God's goodness, trustworthiness, authority, and love. Instead of finding their satisfaction in God alone, Adam and Eve latch onto the forbidden fruit of the tree, their hearts craftily diverted by Satan. He plants the idea in Eve's head that there's more out there for her than what God has given her. Instead of resting and rejoicing in God, she is drawn to the Serpent's table to lust after a forbidden meal. The narrator points out that during this time of temptation, Adam is simply standing by (Gen. 3:6). Most people believe that it was Adam's job to teach his wife of God's important commands. Instead, Adam is a passive spectator.[8] After Eve's appraisal of the tree, she eats its fruit and gives some to Adam, who also indulges (Gen. 3:6). This sin plunges our first parents into death. And with them, all of creation falls into the swirling abyss of sin's curse.

This sin is not restricted to Adam and Eve. All of their children since—indeed all of us—have done the same thing. We have sinned. We have all spurned God's commands. We have all sought to satisfy the desires of our hearts and lusts of our eyes through created things. This is so characteristic of humanity that the apostle Paul uses broad, sweeping, inclusive language to describe it in the New Testament:

> Claiming to be wise, they became fools, and exchanged the glory of the immortal God for images resembling mortal man and birds and animals and creeping things.
>
> . . . they exchanged the truth about God for a lie and worshiped and served the creature rather than the Creator, who is blessed forever! Amen. (Rom. 1:22–23, 25)

The exchange that Paul describes takes place in the human heart. And, like our first parents, we choose to pursue personal contentment in what God has made instead of in God himself. Ultimately this is what sin is. We rebel against God by loving his creation more than we love him. We elevate his good gifts to a place of deity while demoting God to the level of a common thing. We run back to the tree seeking after the magic potion to fill our souls, satisfy our desires, calm our consciences, heal our wounds, and make our lives count. It has never worked.

I remember one relaxing Saturday afternoon at home. In a blur, one of our children ran by me, and it seemed she had something on her face. I called her over and asked what she had eaten. "Noth-

---

8. Even though it was Eve who sinned first (Gen. 3:6), it was Adam whom God pursued (Gen. 3:9), and throughout Scripture it is Adam who is ultimately held responsible (Rom. 5:12) for the first sin. This seems to indicate that Adam did not fulfill his responsibility to lead, instruct, and serve his wife.

ing, Daddy." It was clear that she had gotten into the birthday cake on the counter. The frosting and chocolate betrayed her plea of innocence. So I asked again, and she shamefully put her head down. She knew.

The same is true of us. We fallen human beings are running around with the stains of forbidden fruit all over our faces and hands. Attempting to find the answer to our problems, we only find ourselves more hungry and more saddled with guilt. Everything we touch is smudged with the fingerprints of sin. And everywhere we run, our problem goes with us. Contentment is elusive because sin is pervasive.

Sin never delivers on its promises and always makes things worse. Though we have indulged, we remain empty. What's more, when we sin we feel the guilt. Sin leaves us both hungry and hurting. The rotten fruit of sin has promised the sweet taste of contentment but has delivered bitter misery. Such is the deceptive and destructive work of sin.

How Do We Find Contentment?

I've often been struck by the surprising way God pursued Adam and Eve in the garden of Eden. They were scared and hiding (and rightfully so). The promise of death echoed in their now scorched consciences. They knew what should be coming. We might expect God to act without mercy, unloading his full arsenal of wrath. But he didn't. Instead of turning his back on them, he pursued them. And he pursued them in a way that didn't look at all like the frightful and awesome display that came later on Mount Sinai.

When Moses went up the mountain to meet with God and receive the law, the righteousness of God was demonstrated in thick smoke, thunder, flashes of lightning, and heart-pounding trumpet blasts! (Exodus 19). God spoke to his people out of the midst of a fire! (Deut. 5:24). The scene in the garden was quite different. We read in Genesis 3:9 that God initiated a dialog with the first couple. Graciously and patiently, God talked with them about their sin—even amid their excuse making and blame shifting. Before reading their sentence and pounding the gavel in judgment, God sought out Adam and Eve.

God's pursuit here is important to observe, especially as it sheds light on contentment. He was planning not to destroy them and start over with new people but to speak to them and start over with them. God spoke to them with the same purpose as before—to lead them back to trust God's word and treasure God himself. Or to put it another way, God spoke to them to lead them to contentment in him.

Sin does not draw us to God. Instead it separates us. Like Adam and Eve's response to their shame, our reflex is to hide from and avoid God. But we must not miss the fact that God—without anything to gain personally and out of no other motivation than redemptive love—pursues us. Many people don't worship God because they think they are too good. However, many others don't because they believe they are too bad. This type of thinking will keep people in the shadows, attempting to hide from God in a costume of their own making.

If you believe you are too bad for God, then you must look again at the garden of Eden. God graciously, patiently, and lovingly pursued Adam and Eve with his words of hope and redemption. More than likely they still had the taste of sin in their mouths when they heard the promise of God in their ears. The fact that God pursues bruised reeds like this should deeply encourage us. He pursues us to lead us back to himself. Why? To make us content in him.

The announcement of this pursuit is God's promise to bring salvation through the seed of the woman (Gen. 3:15). Her son will crush the head of the Serpent. This promise is in the kernel in Genesis, but it sprouts and grows, casting a hopeful shadow over the entire Bible. We learn that this rescuer will be the offspring of Abraham (Gen. 12:3), of the tribe of Judah (Gen. 49:10), and a descendant of David (2 Sam. 7:12–16); he will be born of a virgin (Isa. 7:14) in the town of Bethlehem (Mic. 5:2), be sinless (Isa. 53:9, 11), die a substitutionary death (Isa. 53:4–12), and be resurrected (Ps. 16:10). This descendant of Eve, of course, is our Lord Jesus Christ. He is God with us (Isa. 7:14; Matt. 1:22–23).

This is the great story of the Bible: God comes and rescues the hungry, hurting people. Those who have been dispatched in their depravity have been reconciled. God has brought us back to himself (Col. 1:21–22).

Remember the story of the Prodigal Son in Luke 15? Instead of enjoying his status as a son, the young man opted to squander his inheritance through licentiousness (Luke 15:13). He had little regard for his father's love, honor, or support. He was on a mission to splurge, attempting to satisfy his hunger through created things. We know that he hit rock bottom and found himself eating in a pig trough to stave off starvation. So he decided to return home to his father and beg him to accept him as a servant. But to our surprise, as we read the story, we find the father filled with compassion and joy. The dad ran to meet him, hugged him, clothed him in his best robe, and then threw a party for him (Luke 15:22–24). The father joyfully welcomed his son home.

When we read the surrounding passages, we see that there is a theme of rejoicing over the restoration of the lost. Earlier in chapter 15, Jesus tells parables about things that are lost and then found. On two occasions there is abundant rejoicing when what is lost is recovered. In verses 1–7 the rejoicing is over a found sheep. In verses 8–10 the rejoicing is over the lost coin being found. Jesus uses these stories to show us that there is much rejoicing in heaven over one sinner repenting. This sets up the story of the Prodigal Son who repents and returns home. When we repent of our sin and come to faith in Christ, we are coming home to our Father. We are confessing that we have squandered his good gifts by worshiping them instead of him. We are vowing to see God and his world very differently. We are declaring that we will love, serve, and treasure him above all else. We are saying that we will pursue contentment in God alone.

Just as we may not think of Genesis 3 (with its focus on sin) as a passage about discontentment, we may also fail to see conversion as a declaration of our contentment in God. But what else could it mean? We are certainly not saying that when we become Christians, we now find our supreme, soul-settling joy in creation plus God. Conversion is not about adding Jesus to an already crowded shelf of idols.[9] May it never be! Conversion is about sweeping clear the shelves of our heart and pledging supreme love and loyalty to God—and God alone.

Think again about peering over the fence into "the happy land of the Trinity." Informed by Scripture we observe again the overflowing Trinitarian delight amid the perfect reflection and communication of the eternally glorious God. When we become Christians, God welcomes us into this joy. We become partakers of Trinitarian delight. Of course, I don't mean we become members of the Trinity. Instead, we have fellowship with our triune God and therefore become partakers of his joy. This is exactly what prompted the apostle John to be so candid and, at times perhaps, uncomfortably personal in his first epistle. He writes, "That which we have seen and heard we proclaim also to you, so that you too may have fellowship with us; and indeed our fellowship is with the Father and with his Son Jesus Christ. And we are writing these things so that our joy may be complete" (1 John 1:3–4).

We should remember that this is precisely what Jesus prayed for in his High Priestly Prayer: "But now I am coming to you, and these things I speak in the world, that they may have my joy fulfilled in themselves" (John 17:13). The apostle Peter spoke of the "inexpressible joy" that comes from truly knowing God: "Though you have not seen him, you love him. Though you do not now see him, you believe in him and rejoice with joy that is inexpressible

---

9. In other words, I am not saying that conversion is about accommodating the ongoing breaking of the first commandment, "You shall have no other gods before me" (Ex. 20:3).

and filled with glory" (1 Pet. 1:8). This joy, then, is tough to pin down with earthly terms. In fact, that seems to be Peter's point; it is joy from another land! We don't really have words to capture the hues and textures of this joy—it is heavenly!

Jonathan Edwards wrote in his *Religious Affections*[10] that this joy is unspeakable in both kind and degree. In *kind* it is unlike any "worldly joys" or "carnal delights." Edwards wrote that it is "of a vastly more pure, sublime, and heavenly nature, being something supernatural, and truly divine, and so ineffably excellent; the sublimity and exquisite sweetness of which, there were no words to set forth."[11] This joy is absolutely different from anything else we have come to know as common in this world.

But this joy is also, according to Edwards, unspeakable in *degree*. We should be amazed not only that God has given us this heavenly joy but also that he has been pleased to give it to us "with a liberal hand and in large measure."[12] He has not simply put a drop of it upon our thirsty tongues, but he has dumped the Gatorade bucket over our heads through the gospel! We have been lavished with heavenly joy through our experience of fellowship in the gospel.

The incarnation, death, and resurrection of Jesus Christ form a beautiful, multifaceted diamond. It has countless heart-stirring implications. However, we must not miss this central truth: it is a Trinitarian priority for Christians to know and experience the overflowing joy that comes from the gospel. Contentment is the abiding "Amen" of our joy. It speaks in the present tense, saying, "I am tasting and I am seeing that the Lord is good." In a similar vein, Thomas Chalmers wrote of the "expulsive power of a new affection." This means that the gospel brings us to something and someone greater than what we previously desired. The new affection of love for Christ drives out the dull, old desires and replaces

---

10. Jonathan Edwards, *A Treatise concerning Religious Affections: In Three Parts* . . . (Oak Harbor, WA: Logos Research Systems, 1996), 2.
11. Ibid. 2.
12. Ibid.

them with the riches of Christ. These riches are ours through the gospel of Christ.

A Four-Dimensional World

Sinclair Ferguson helpfully describes contentment in God as four dimensions of knowing Christ.[13]

Dimension 1. "Everything we need and everything we lack is found in Christ." When we truly grasp and experience this truth, it is a game changer. Echoing Edwards, Ferguson warns against merely having the "notion" of this sufficiency in Christ. Too many "have the idea, but the reality does not touch our affections."[14] All Christians would say that we are saved by Christ alone, but still they often seek happiness, identity, and purpose elsewhere. When we realize that the gospel has brought us home to God, we realize too that he has brought us there by the all-sufficient Christ.

Dimension 2. "This all-sufficient Christ is with us." This truth of Christ's sufficiency is not simply a theory; it is an abiding reality. He comes and abides with us. The force behind the exhortation to be content (Heb. 13:5–6) is the truth that God will never leave nor forsake his people. "The Greek text here contains an entire handful of negatives—bad in English grammar, permissible in Greek, but glorious in theology. The message is: this all-sufficient Lord Jesus is with you; no way will He leave you. This is all you need."[15] This is powerful truth. We don't have to look elsewhere, for Christ is with us.

Dimension 3. "We are in this all-sufficient Christ." This means that we are united to Christ. The union of Christ to his people is a legal and a spiritual union. Legally, we stand on Christ's merit, and spiritually we enjoy communion with the triune God. To be in Christ means that "we are united to him in the eternal counsel, in the federal union, by his incarnation and through faith."[16]

---

13. Sinclair Ferguson, "Our New Affection," *Tabletalk*, December 2015, 22.
14. Ibid.
15. Ibid.
16. Ibid.

Dimension 4. "This all-sufficient Christ is in us." Though we still sin, we have the privilege of Christ living in us (Gal. 2:20). God the Holy Spirit has come to make his home with us (John 14:17, 20, 23b; 17:23).[17]

\- \- \-

At the beginning of the chapter we asked, "Why should we be content in God?" The answer is threefold: because this is what we were created to be, this is what Christ died to make us, and this is the privilege of those who are indwelt by God the Spirit. God's design for us to be captivated and calibrated by his glory was once lost because of sin, but now has been won through the gospel. We become content by trusting in the God who is content.

Review Questions

1. Why is it crucial to understand that God is content in himself?

2. What role does our perversion of God's gifts play in our discontentment?

3. Identify three good gifts of God that you find yourself worrying about.

4. How does the gospel lead us back to God as the source and sustainer of our contentment?

5. Do you believe the statement "Everything we need and everything we lack is found in Christ"? Why is the answer to this so important?

---

17. Ibid.

Part 2

LEARNING CONTENTMENT

3

Better Than I Deserve

Over a period of several months I noticed, while we were singing at church, that the words on the screen were a bit out of focus. I would think, *I wish we could get that to sharpen up.* Every now and then I'd consider mentioning it to the people who set up the slides, but figuring it sounded petty, I'd just forget about it.

One week, however, I was pleasantly surprised. In the middle of the first song, I couldn't believe my eyes. The letters were crisp. *This is great*, I thought; *and I hadn't said a thing.* Filled with the joy that comes from the unexpected small victories in life, I turned toward the balcony to see who was running the slides. I wanted to encourage that person after the service for the good work. But as I looked, my brand-new glasses were sliding down my nose, and I had to adjust them. Suddenly it hit me: it wasn't the slides at all. It was me all along! My eyes had been getting progressively worse, and that's why the words on the screen had become more and more fuzzy. It was only when I put on my glasses that I was able to see properly—and not just the world around me, but also my own condition. I was the problem!

This story illustrates what happens when we are given sight through the gospel. Suddenly we recognize that our central problem is not other people or the conditions around us. It is our own spiritual blindness to the glory of God and to our innumerable and exceedingly heinous sins. We discover that God has been very kind to us, giving us far better than we deserve. Instead of wrath, judgment, and eternal hopelessness, we are given mercy and life and eyes to see! Contentment comes through the lenses of the gospel.

At the very beginning of his *Institutes of the Christian Religion*, John Calvin makes a couple of profound observations. At first glance they seem to contradict each other, but as we consider them, they are bound together as foundational truths. Calvin says that without knowing ourselves, we could not possibly come to know God. "We cannot seriously aspire to him before we begin to become displeased with ourselves."[1] In other words, fundamental to knowledge of God is a biblical knowledge of self that includes being repulsed by our sin. The complementary principle seems at first to contradict the first one. Calvin goes on to develop his point that without a true knowledge of God, we cannot really know ourselves.

How can these two go together? How can we not truly know ourselves without knowing God *and* not truly know God without knowing ourselves? The answer is that the Bible reveals both forms of knowledge. The Bible teaches us who God is and who we are. In chapter 2 we discussed God's character at length. Pushing off of these truths, we know that God is the Creator, and therefore he sets the rules as the authority. Because he is holy, righteous, and good, he must maintain his honor in response to all who oppose him. God is unchanging in his holiness, righteousness, and goodness, and he will act in accordance with this character. And this means that we have to think about our sin. As Calvin teaches, when we see these two properly—knowledge of God's character and knowledge of ourselves—we make true gains in the pursuit of godliness.

---

1. John Calvin, *Institutes of the Christian Religion*, ed. John T. McNeill, trans. Ford Lewis Battles (Louisville: Westminster John Knox, 2001), 1.1.1.

Understanding Our Sin

Proper understanding of our sin leads to an abiding gratitude toward God for his mercy. Because this is crucial to learning contentment, let's look at a few specifics.

What is sin? Sin is described in several different ways in the New Testament: missing the mark (Rom. 3:23), stepping across the line (Col. 2:13), trespassing or falling (Matt. 6:14), lawlessness (1 John 3:4), and debt (Matt. 6:12). God has a standard of what is right and acceptable to him. Sin is the rebellious violation of this standard. If that sounds a tad abstract, let's get personal.

Sin is so bad because of who it is against. We come to understand these ways of describing sin when we see them in light of who God is. We are missing *God's* mark. We are stepping across *God's* line. We are breaking *God's* law. While our sin does have horizontal implications, we must remember that sin is, before anything else, against God. David expressed this when he cried out to God in his prayer of confession,

> Against you, you only, have I sinned
>   and done what is evil in your sight. (Ps. 51:4)

This might strike us as odd, because we are familiar with the story behind this confession. David had sex with a woman who was not his wife, had her husband murdered, covered it up, and went about his business. It seems in this story that there were few people he *didn't* sin against. Yet he directed his cry for mercy to God. David understood that above all, his sin was against God. Sin is always theological and it's always personal. When we sin, we sin against God. This is what makes it so bad.

Sin is so bad because it is so widespread. Sin impacts every single person every single day. Whether we speak of guilt, shame, fear, mourning, or anxiety—everything comes from a cursed world. Sin is a pervasive and persistent epidemic. It affects all of us. We all know its pain. We have all felt its consequences. And yet we are all responsible.

Sin is so bad because its penalty is so certain and severe. The Bible tells us that "the wages of sin is death" (Rom. 6:23). The required payment for sin is death. Because sin is primarily against God, it requires a sufficient judgment. This is one reason why Jesus described hell as "eternal fire" (Matt. 25:41). Sin is an infinite offense against an infinitely glorious God. As a result, hell is the eternal demonstration and execution of God's infinite justice. In hell God is punishing man's infinite rebellion with infinite wrath. This severe penalty is packaged as the certain wages of sin (Rom. 6:23).

Sin is so bad because we have no way to remedy it ourselves. To make matters worse we have no means to get ourselves out of this predicament. Everywhere we turn to help ourselves, we leave more fingerprints of sin. Even if we could somehow obey God's law perfectly going forward, we would have no means to remove our previous sentence of judgment. In and of ourselves we are stuck.

Mercy Makes Us Sing

As a pastor, I have the blessing of sitting down and talking with many people about their relationship with God. If they are Christians, I'm often privileged to hear them retell the circumstances that God used to bring them to faith in Christ. I'm deeply affected by the way a believer's eyes tell the story along with his or her words. Often, as people talk about the Lord's kind and patient mercy, their eyes well up with tears. Those tears mark moments of clarity—for me and the one speaking. They remind us of the ultimate priorities in life. The truth is, we deserve hell and we got mercy! Certainly you can see how this would inform our understanding of contentment. When you deserve hell, anything else is cause for celebration!

I'm convinced that this was key for the apostle Paul's pursuit of contentment. Let's remember that he confessed he could be content with much or little (Phil. 4:11–12). He demonstrated this by singing and praying while chained in a Philippian jail (Acts 16).

What makes you sing amid extremely difficult circumstances? It is an awareness of a greater reality.

> The saying is trustworthy and deserving of full acceptance, that Christ Jesus came into the world to save sinners, of whom I am the foremost. But I received mercy for this reason, that in me, as the foremost, Jesus Christ might display his perfect patience as an example to those who were to believe in him for eternal life. (1 Tim. 1:15–16)

Paul understood that all people have sinned and fallen short of the glory of God (Rom. 3:23). There are none who are righteous, who seek God, or who fear him (Rom. 3:9–18). All of humanity is quarantined under sin. Left to ourselves, we are helpless and hopeless. We should notice that when Paul considered that army of rebellion against God, he saw himself not simply among the ranks but in the front line. He called himself the foremost, or chief, of sinners.

Paul was a guy who understood the depths of his depravity. We see this starkly when we read through the book of Acts. In chapter 8, during the execution of Stephen, Paul (formerly Saul of Tarsus) was standing by approving of the malicious violence (8:1). Furthermore, he was a vigilant persecutor of the church: "But Saul was ravaging the church, and entering house after house, he dragged off men and women and committed them to prison" (8:3). In fact, we must not forget that he was on his way to Damascus when he was converted by Christ. He was an enemy of the cross who came to love the cross. As Saul was seeking to arrest Christians, he found himself arrested by Christ! The King showed him mercy, and he never got over it.

As you think of how Saul was radically converted and became our beloved apostle Paul, you may be tempted to keep some mental distance from him. "I can see why mercy was on the front burner for Paul. How could he ever forget a past like that?" Many people think this way and, as a result, minimize the mercy they've received. If a key component of learning contentment is remembering the mercy we've been shown, we must take care to identify any potential hindrances to the practice.

Hindrances to Realizing Mercy

Relativizing Sin

It's very tempting to utter a quiet "Amen" to the cultural sermons proclaimed around us. When many people think about sin today, they think in terms of the extreme end of the scale. Sin is what Hitler or Bin Laden did. We, in contrast, make "mistakes." And our mistakes are not really that bad. When we begin to feel the sting of sin and the weight of conviction, we are met with cultural litigators vying to represent us. We turn on the TV and see our peers doing worse things. We watch the news and hear of those in the highest offices involved in all levels of corruption. We learn of sports heroes who are caught up in greed and selfishness. We often talk not in terms of what is right and wrong but what is common. "We all make mistakes." While this is true, Christians must guard against relativizing sin and emptying it of its meaning.

As Christians we understand that the very fact that we have sinned against God proves our desperate need for mercy. And it was God, moved by love, who demonstrated such pardoning mercy through Christ. When we think about sin, we must be sure to remember its biblical weight and context. Sin is so bad because of who it is against. And sin is so pressing because apart from Christ we have no remedy for its debt. To relativize sin is to deflate mercy. This type of thinking will erode contentment.

Forgetting Our Ultimate Need

Scott would sit in the front pew each week at our Sunday gathering. Over time his medical condition continued to get worse, but he rarely missed church. Each week, after the benediction, people would come up and talk with him. When they did, especially in the last months of his life, they would find a man who was increasingly frail. Though he was only in his early forties, his body was breaking down. After transplants, an amputation, and years in and out of the hospital, Scott was nearing the end of his earthly life.

One Sunday morning I was able to get to him before others did. I had preached from Habakkuk about trusting God even when life doesn't make sense. Scott grabbed my hand with all the strength he could muster and, with eyes full of tears, said, "Erik, pray for me. I am so selfish. I forget how good God has been to me. He has taken away my sin and given me Christ—what else do I need? Pray that I don't forget it this week." That was one of the last times he would be able to come to church. Soon he would gather with the saints above in heaven, rather than the saints below on earth.

Do you see how practical this doctrine of mercy was for Scott? At his funeral a number of people spoke of how remarkable it was that even amid such bodily affliction he maintained such a positive outlook. To some it may have seemed like he was a strong-minded guy. I knew better. After seven years of watching Scott grow in grace, I knew he was strong—but not like most thought. He was made strong by becoming weak. He was strengthened by the grace of Christ. And the way he was fed was by the tender mercy of God. He was content because he understood and experienced mercy.

Thinking We're Awesome

Living as a Christian entails an honest reckoning of our strengths and weaknesses. Have you ever sat down and just thought about the essence of the Christian life? At its core, it truly is a pride-smashing worldview. We are basically admitting that we've messed it up and need a new start.

When I was a seventh grader, we would play a foolish game between classes. Our school building was constructed in the early 1900s and had large radiators on the side of each room. As immature young men, we would grab ahold of the radiators in the wintertime and see who could hold on the longest. Some guys would position their hands real close to the pipes and not really grasp them. Veterans of the game would call them out, "Grab ahold of it!" When truly grasped by even the strongest twelve-year-olds, the pipes would quickly become too hot. Pride would vanish and hands would let go.

When you and I truly grab hold of Christ, pride plays a different role. It wants us to let go and be self-sufficient. In ourselves, we cannot hold on. The refining word of truth is simply too hot. But through that very gospel, God's Spirit melts away our pride. We come to grips with Christ by the Spirit's grip on us.

The reality is that the qualification for entry into the kingdom of God is weakness, not strength. Walk through the gospel narratives and contrast the reception Jesus gives those who are weak with his response to those who appear to be strong.[2] There has to be an awareness of personal weakness and Christ's sufficiency before anyone can even begin to appreciate and understand Jesus. When questioned by the grumbling religious leaders about his methodology, Jesus replied: "Those who are well have no need of a physician, but those who are sick. I came not to call the righteous, but sinners" (Mark 2:17).

The point is clear: Jesus came for weak people who are looking for someone strong to lean upon in faith. He did not come for apparently strong people who are looking for congratulations on their awesomeness. Therefore, whether we are talking about kingdom entrance (conversion) or kingdom living (our Christian life), Christianity is about strength—just not our own.

Moving on Too Quickly

I hope you are beginning to see the importance of having a proper biblical understanding of sin. But we need to do more than understand it. For example, let's say you're a parent and you've become

---

2. This contrast is seen clearly in Mark's Gospel. Weak and helpless people include lepers (1:40–45), paralytics (2:1–13), a man with the withered hand (3:1–5), the demoniac, Jairus's daughter, and the woman with the hemorrhage (5:1–43). The apparently strong are Pharisees and religious leaders (2:1–28; 7:1–23).

discontent because you've pinned much of your identity on your kid's success. In time your fragile dream is crushed when your realize that your child is not perfect and, in fact, is getting into some trouble. By God's grace you are convicted of placing too much hope in your child rather than in God. You rightly identify the sin of selfishness in making a little idol of yourself in your children rather than forming Christ in them. You see how it is wrong and hurting you, and you repent. You wash your hands and move on.

But is that all? Don't we have a tendency to move on too quickly from our sin and as a result miss some tremendous blessings in the process? The eighteenth-century English Puritan John Owen wrote extensively on the topic of sin and temptation. In one section he warned against this common practice of moving on too fast. Owen cautioned against simply agreeing that something is wrong without being affected by how wrong it is. He writes, "Bring the holy law of God into your conscience, lay your corruption to it, pray that you may be affected with it. Consider the holiness, spirituality, fiery severity, inwardness, absoluteness of the law, and see how you can stand before it."[3]

Owen was basically advocating that we work on the entire engine of the conscience while the hood is up. The proper work of the law is "to discover sin in the guilt of it, to awake and humble the soul for it . . ."[4] Before moving on from the conviction of sin, the Christian is encouraged to shine the light of God's Word into the nooks and crannies of the conscience. Let it expose the cobwebs and other neglected quarters so as to bring proper conviction. This is like power washing the conscience with the hydro-force of the law. It cleanses by focused energy.

There is a second step that must not be neglected, according to Owen. He teaches us to bring our lust to the gospel. When we read this we might say, "Finally, some relief." But Owen basically says, "Not so fast":

3. John Owen, *Temptation and Sin* (Evansville, IN: Sovereign Grace, 1958), 57.
4. Ibid.

Bring *thy lust to the gospel*,—not for relief, but for farther conviction of its guilt; look on Him whom thou hast pierced, and be in bitterness. Say to thy soul, "What have I done? What love, what mercy, what blood, what grace have I despised and trampled on! Is this the return I make to the Father for his *love*, to the Son for his *blood*, to the Holy Ghost for his *grace*? Do I thus requite the Lord? Have I defiled the heart that Christ died to wash, that the blessed Spirit hath chosen to dwell in? And can I keep myself out of the dust? What can I say to the dear Lord Jesus? How shall I hold up my head with any boldness before him? Do I account communion with him of so little value, that for this vile lust's sake I have scarce left him any room in my heart? How shall I escape if I neglect so great salvation? In the meantime, what shall I say to the Lord? Love, mercy, grace, goodness, peace, joy, consolation,—I have despised them all, and esteemed them as a thing of nought, that I might harbour a lust in my heart. Have I obtained a view of God's fatherly countenance, that I might behold his face and provoke him to his face? Was my soul washed, that room might be made for new defilements? Shall I endeavour to disappoint the end of the death of Christ? Shall I daily grieve that Spirit whereby I am sealed to the day of redemption?" Entertain thy conscience daily with this treaty.[5]

John Owen helps us here as a doctor of sanctification. He cautions us about moving too quickly from sin to the banquet table of forgiveness. He is attempting to produce in us contrite, humble, grateful hearts. Therefore, after doing the appropriate "law work" and contemplating our sin in light of the gospel, he instructs us to descend further into the particulars of our sin in light of the benefits of the gospel. "Consider," says Owen, "the infinite patience and forbearance of God."[6] We should not take God's mercy for granted. As Christians, we should be familiar with mercy but

---

5. Ibid., 58.
6. Ibid.

never presume upon it. Mercy is a costly divine gift that should inflame our hearts with love even as it melts our pride.

If the realization of mercy helps the Christian to learn contentment, then the extra work prescribed by Owen deepens that realization. Don't move on too quickly, but descend low into the recesses of your conscience to clear away the cobwebs and refresh your soul in divine love.

Missing the Point of the Trial

In our home we have six children. As you can imagine, this brings a parade of child-training opportunities. In addition to the blessing of children, the Lord has blessed me with a wife who is very creative and persistent in how she trains the kids.

Not surprisingly, young children will sometimes do things they shouldn't. Let's say they're playing Dora the Explorer Chutes and Ladders. One child snatches the backpack piece, because he wants to be the backpack and not the monkey. Another child becomes upset. As parents we intervene, explain the wrong behavior, show why it is wrong, and show them the right way to handle the situation ("We don't snatch with our hands but ask nicely with our mouths"). Then we'll make them redo the entire sequence to make sure the lesson is learned and the right behavior is modeled. Believe it or not, sometimes the kids will only go through the motions—they won't really buy in. When this happens, my patient and committed wife will start over, explaining, modeling, and redoing the right behavior. I have seen this go on a half dozen times before the child seems to get it. Here is a parent who is willing to take the time to teach her kids.

I'm convinced that God often uses trials for the same purpose. Through repetition he brings us to see what is really important while training us in godliness. The fifth chapter of James addresses believers in the midst of persistent trials. James urges them to patiently endure the difficulty (5:7–8). He reminds them that patience and perseverance through trials are the traits of the faithful throughout history (5:10–11). And then he assures them that the Lord is compassionate and merciful (5:11).

Often adversity is a tool of the Lord to remove the things that impede our contentment. The point of the trial is to clarify our vision, strengthen our faith, and produce perseverance (James 1:3). In this process we are reminded of the truth that God is compassionate toward us. No matter how difficult a situation is, we cannot outrun the abiding truth that God has been merciful to us. Being reminded of God's mercy clears away discontentment by assuring us that God is for us in Christ Jesus—even if we must "redo" a trial a few times before we get the message.

– – –

If you are having a hard time being content, make a list of everything you have that you don't deserve, and then make a list of everything you deserve that you don't have. When you and I realize how kind and gracious God has been with us, we're able to see things in a proper perspective.

Do you remember when you were first converted? Mercy and love flowed down from heaven through the words of the gospel. You were forgiven and accepted. What glorious truth! God had taken care of your most pressing problem, and he had taken care of it powerfully and permanently.

We have been shown tremendous mercy. We have cried, with the sinner in the temple, "God be merciful to me, the sinner!" and God has answered with infinite mercy. When we remember that our ultimate and most pressing need is fully met in him, it is very difficult to complain. As I've heard Mark Dever quip, "Anything less than hell is dancing time for Christians!" Amen. May we never forget it.

Review Questions

1. Why is it so important that we understand who God is in order to rightly understand who we are?

2. List some synonyms for these words: *sin*, *mercy*, *grace*, and *salvation*.

3. What is the relationship between understanding your sin and esteeming God's grace?

4. What are some hindrances to our appreciation of God's mercy?

5. How does the quote "Anything less than hell is dancing time for Christians!" relate to your contentment? Do you believe this?

4

Left, Right, Left . . .

When I was eighteen years old, I joined the military. I wish I could say I joined out of a sense of duty or patriotism, but I did not. I was a rebellious, unreliable, irresponsible kid. Evidently I was just the type of kid they were looking for, because I soon found myself surrounded by dozens of like-minded "brothers." The training instructors (TIs) had a plan, though. They had six weeks to shape some raw material into productive members of the military. They were going to create an identity, pride, a work ethic, and responsibility. I can't look back without some degree of astonishment. They actually did it, after all.

What is interesting is *how* they did it. The TIs were intent on teaching recruits to pay close attention to detail and take pride in their work. Under the pressure of looming inspections, we spent hours folding our clothes according to the standards. (I still remember using a paperclip to get the edges perfect.) We shined our boots, made our beds, and cleaned our barracks meticulously. Everywhere we went we marched. Whether in a group of fifty guys or in twos, we were always marching and always pivoting right or left just like we were supposed to. We did this day after day and week after week.

Eventually I graduated and moved on to further training. I realized something strange had happened, though. I shined my boots daily, called everyone sir or ma'am, and folded my laundry with precision. If my parents could have seen the transformation over a few months, they would not have believed their eyes. I truly was a different guy.

But there's more. I was also quite excited about being part of the military. It was more than a paycheck or another job; it became something I cared deeply about. Over a period of several weeks the TIs had done the seemingly impossible. They had taken an indifferent, uncommitted recruit and transformed him into a productive and committed member of the military. Their routines and repetition had brought about their desired end.

What is the goal of the Christian life? The answer to the first question of the Westminster Shorter Catechism says it best: "to glorify God and to enjoy him forever." To glorify God is to make much of him, to see his supreme value and ascribe greatness to him. But we do more than agree that God is great. We enter into the hearty "Amen!" of his greatness by living in such a way that testifies to the fact that God is our supreme treasure and surpassing joy. To use the analogy of the military, we live in such a way that properly reflects the honor and glory of the one who has enlisted us into service.

How do we glorify God and enjoy him forever? We glorify God by learning, tasting, seeing, and showing that the Lord is glorious. We come to find ourselves in hearty agreement with God that he is worthy of our whole-souled devotion. This is precisely what we have been thinking about in terms of learning contentment. Being content in God is being satisfied in God regardless of what is going on outside you.

The biblical argument is that you cannot truly be content without being content in God. The apostle Paul highlights this indissoluble bond between godliness and contentment in 1 Timothy 6. He says there that false teachers were "imagining that godliness

is a means of gain. But godliness with contentment is great gain"
(6:5–6). In this section of the letter, Paul is unmasking the false
teachers by exposing their works. These opponents to true religion
are "puffed up" with conceit, ignorant, and craving controversies.
What's more, they believe that godliness can be a vehicle for personal gain. Regrettably, every age has seen selfish people attempt
to personally capitalize on the church. But, says Paul, this is just
another demonstration of a deceitful, self-inclined heart. Such
schemes don't work. They can't work, because contentment is tied
to godliness after all.

Think about it. Contentment is tied to godliness. At the risk
of trivializing this point, I'm reminded of a bumper sticker I've
seen: "Know Jesus, know peace. No Jesus, no peace." It's a clever
and true turn of phrase. And the same can be said for contentment: "No godliness, no contentment. Know godliness, know
contentment."

Do you see how ironic Paul's correction of the false teachers
is? He basically throws their words back at them with an opposite
meaning. The false teachers believe that godliness is a way to gain.
They are dead wrong, but they are also spot-on. They are wrong
in the way they are going about it, "merchandising the doctrine of
Christ," says Calvin;[1] however, if we do think about it, there is no
true and lasting gain *apart from* godliness. So if we are after gain,
then we actually have to pursue godliness. The key here is what
we mean by "gain." John Stott explains:

> "Godliness" (*eusebeia*) is "gain" (*porismos*), even *great gain*
> ([1 Tim. 6:]6a), providing you mean spiritual gain, not finan-
> cial, and providing you add *contentment*. Paul is echoing his
> earlier statement that "godliness has value for all things,"
> bringing blessing for both this life and the next ([1 Tim.] 4:8).[2]

1. John Calvin, *Commentaries on the Epistles to Timothy, Titus, and Philemon*, trans.
William Pringle (Bellingham, WA: Logos Bible Software, 2010), 157.
2. John R. W. Stott, *Guard the Truth: The Message of 1 Timothy & Titus*, The Bible
Speaks Today (Downers Grove, IL: InterVarsity Press, 1996), 149.

The apostle hits his mark. Godliness is concerned not primarily with the physical, expressed in terms of money, but with the spiritual, expressed in terms of contentment.

We must see how revolutionary this line of thinking is. As we saw earlier, in Paul's day Stoic philosophers taught that people could achieve a self-sufficiency that would insulate them from the tumultuous circumstances of life (see under the heading "Contentment Is a Work of Grace," p. 27). By looking inward and mastering themselves, they attempted to ensure that they were unmovable, unflappable, stoic. In fact, here in 1 Timothy 6:6 Paul uses the same word that was commonly used by the Stoics. The difference for Paul, however, is not the end (contentment) but the means to that end. Whereas the Stoics pursued sufficiency in themselves, we as Christians find it in God. Thomas Lea and Hayne Griffin comment: "Paul Christianized the term, using it to refer to an attitude of mind independent of externals and dependent only on God. He was not advocating godless self-sufficiency as a source of contentment. Paul believed that true sufficiency is Christ-sufficiency (Phil. 4:13)."[3]

In our day, we don't often look inward to master ourselves but look outward to satisfy ourselves. If we can only get more and enjoy more, then we'll be happy. However, research shows that even those who seem to have the most still lack contentment. They have hands full of money but happiness slips through their eager grasp. In a study conducted by Boston College, researchers talked with people whose fortunes exceeded $25 million. The goal of the study was to get the rich to speak candidly about their lives. According to the study,

> The respondents turn out to be a generally dissatisfied lot, whose money has contributed to deep anxieties involving love, work, and family. Indeed, they are frequently dissatisfied even with their sizable fortunes. Most of them still do not consider themselves financially secure; for that, they say, they would

---

3. Thomas D. Lea and Hayne P. Griffin, *1, 2 Timothy, Titus*, The New American Commentary 34 (Nashville: Broadman & Holman, 1992), 167–68.

require on average one-quarter more wealth than they currently possess.[4]

Here are people who seem to have made it. They are in the cultural winner's circle but don't feel victorious.

Paul exposes this same type of emptiness in the next verses of 1 Timothy 6. He goes on to point out that even if you get a lot of stuff, you can't keep it. We are all going to die eventually, and our stuff will not come with us or help us in the age to come (6:7). Further, instead of providing contentment, the pursuit of riches can often provide a snare, a vicious temptation that ends in ruin (6:9).

Whether we look inward or outward, we see that promises for gain are actually empty promises. Contentment comes not from focusing on ourselves or feasting on stuff but by focusing and feasting on Jesus Christ (Phil. 4:13). Contentment comes through knowing *and* loving the truth. It is not enough to simply know theology; we must love the God we are studying. And it is not enough to say we love a God we do not know. Godliness is concerned with both knowing and loving.

How then do we do this? How do we grow in godliness and experience this abiding contentment? Just as the military makes and trains soldiers through (monotonous but nevertheless purposeful) repetition, so too God grows his people through specific personal practices. We often refer to these practices as spiritual disciplines. Let's think together how these disciplines help us focus and feast upon Christ. And in so doing, we will be learning the art of contentment.

Bible Reading

Jesus prayed for his followers to grow in holiness. What is the means of this growth? It is the Word of God. Jesus prayed, "Sanctify them in the truth; your word is truth" (John 17:17). God uses

---

4. Graeme Wood, "Secret Fears of the Super-Rich," *The Atlantic*, April 2011, http://www.theatlantic.com/magazine/archive/2011/04/secret-fears-of-the-super-rich/308419.

the Scripture to mold us into Christlikeness (2 Cor. 3:18). It only makes sense that the Word that gives us life also gives shape to our life. God's Word forms and transforms us as Christians.

In Psalm 19 we find several descriptions of God's Word that compel us to read it. The first is that it is perfect (19:7). The Bible lacks nothing that we need; it is fully sufficient. This draws us to it for instruction and training. Commenting on this verse Matthew Henry observes, "It [God's law] is perfectly free from all corruption, perfectly filled with all good, and perfectly fitted for the end for which it is designed; and it will make the man of God perfect, 2 Tim. 3:17. Nothing is to be added to it nor taken from it."[5]

Also in Psalm 19:7 we see that this perfect Word is suitable to revive the soul. The psalmist is talking about the inner you, the part of you that never dies. The Bible revives you. It is a life-giving and a life-sustaining word. Luther described this reviving: "The Word of God refreshes, revives, and comforts the weak, burdened, and disturbed consciences that were previously troubled by the multiplicity of works and worship."[6] Calvin made the connection "that as the soul gives vigour and strength to the body, so the law in like manner is the life of the soul."[7] In other words, it is God's Word that nourishes and sustains us as believers. It continues to be the agent that scrubs, purifies, and cleanses us. Like a sacred power washer, it blasts away the mold and mildew of sin that accumulates through our ordinary, day-to-day life. The Word cleanses us as it makes us holy.

The psalmist goes on to say that the Scriptures are "sure, making wise the simple" (19:7). This word "sure" means that God's Word is trustworthy; it is faithful. Calvin comments, "When we give ourselves up to be guided and governed by the word of God,

5. Matthew Henry, *Matthew Henry's Commentary on the Whole Bible: Complete and Unabridged in One Volume* (Peabody, MA: Hendrickson, 1994), 768.
6. Martin Luther, *Selected Psalms I*, vol. 12 of *Luther's Works*, ed. Jaroslav Pelikan, Hilton C. Oswald, and Helmut T. Lehmann (St. Louis, MO: Concordia, 1999), 142.
7. John Calvin, *Commentary on the Book of Psalms*, vol. 1, trans. James Anderson (Bellingham, WA: Logos Bible Software, 2010), 319.

we are in no danger of going astray, since this is the path by which he securely guides his own people to salvation."[8]

I remember when my son first started driving; I meticulously gave him directions of how to meet us later in the day. He was going to be driving through some unfamiliar and frankly dangerous areas; I wanted to ensure that he knew where he was going. Our Lord, ever the loving and caring Father, provides us with the trustworthy directions for navigating this life. Our job is to hear and heed him.

Notice what this perfect, sure, and right Word does. It makes wise the simple (19:7). The term "simple" refers to the young or immature—the undiscerning. David's point is that we all come to God as dependent children who need to grow in our godliness. We need to have our minds renewed and reformed to think God's thoughts after him. One of the main hindrances to giving ourselves to regular reading and study of the Scriptures is the folly of thinking that we are wise. Rather, God would have us become fools (1 Cor. 3:18) that we would become wise in him through the instruction of the Bible.

Certainly you can see how a regular reading of God's Word would aid our pursuit of contentment. If our main problem is that we devalue God and overvalue created things (Rom. 1:21–23), then the Bible would graciously loosen our idolatrous grip upon this world by inclining our hearts to see God as our surpassing joy. The Bible shows both the truth and the treasure of God. He is trustworthy and treasure worthy! Look at what the psalmist says:

The precepts of the LORD are right,
    rejoicing the heart. (Ps. 19:8)

More to be desired are they than gold,
    even much fine gold;
sweeter also than honey
    and drippings of the honeycomb. (Ps. 19:10)

---

8. Ibid.

The Scriptures are delicious to the souls of Christians and placed in stark contrast to the natural pursuits of men. We are inclined toward money (gold) and pleasure (delight). But here we see that the law of God is an inexhaustible treat for our spiritual taste buds. In the Bible we are taught who God is even as we are reminded that he is our God. Being reminded that God is truly awesome and gracious to us drives us to refasten our grip on him in faith and live in humble obedience to him.

Certainly you are aware that simply reading the Bible will not make you content in God. Countless people throughout history have read their Bibles regularly without true belief. Even the Pharisees in Jesus's time were known to have memorized large portions of the Scriptures. Exposure to the Word of God does not guarantee a love for it.

As a pastor I get to visit with many Christians who are trying to grow in their understanding and application of the Scriptures. I often hear of their regret that when they do read the Bible in the morning, they often forget what they've read by lunchtime.

This reminds me of my visits to the dentist as a kid. After all the dentist's picking and cleaning, I would be given fluoride. I'd choose a flavor, apply the gushy material, and then spit it out. The hygienist would then treat me like a prizefighter and squirt water into my mouth. Compliantly, I'd swish and spit. Then I'd be done, out of the chair, and on my way out the door.

Too many of us practice dental-chair devotions. We grab our Bibles, spend some time in them, and then we are done. We promptly put down our Bibles and hurry on to our daily tasks. A few hours later someone could ask, "What did you read in the Word today?" And the answer, too often, would be "I can't remember."

What has happened? We've grabbed a little Bible reading, swished it around in the morning, then spit it out on our way out the door. The treasures of the Word haven't been swallowed and digested. We haven't really engaged the mind and heart with the Word.

How we read the Bible is pivotal to our pursuit of contentment. After all, contentment is learned by growth in grace. And
remember, contentment is the inward, gracious, quiet spirit that
joyfully rests in God's providence. To get there, we can't simply go
through the motions; we need to resist "swish and spit" devotions.
Here are some practices I've found helpful.

Pray before You Read

Since contentment is a spiritual work, it would make sense not to
trust the arm of the flesh but to trust the God of grace. Therefore,
it is biblical to come to God in prayer when we are reading the
Scriptures. In *When I Don't Desire God*, John Piper advises Christians to pray four specific requests before coming to the Bible, and
he has developed the helpful acronym IOUS to remember them:[9]

- *Incline* my heart to you, not to prideful gain or any false
  motive (Ps. 119:36).
- *Open* my eyes to behold wonderful things in your Word
  (Ps. 119:18).
- *Unite* my heart to fear your name (Ps. 86:11).
- *Satisfy* me with your steadfast love (Ps. 90:14).

Prayer before we read the Bible expresses anticipation that we
will be affected by it. It is as if we are saying on the front end: "I
am not going through the motions. I need help in this battle for
contentment. Your Word is my food. Feed me and satisfy me with
your perfect Word."

Meditate upon God's Word

I remember, shortly after my conversion, hearing a pastor preach
about meditation. I admit that for most of the sermon I was a bit
lost. I couldn't get past my biblically illiterate concept of meditation. I pictured a certain pose, a particular kind of breathing, and

---

9. See John Piper, *When I Don't Desire God: How to Fight for Joy* (Wheaton, IL: Crossway, 2004), 151–52.

an emptying of the mind. It made no sense why a Christian needed to do this.

In his book *Spiritual Disciplines for the Christian Life*, Don Whitney helpfully clarifies the matter:

> Meditation is not folding your arms, leaning back in your chair, and staring at the ceiling. That's daydreaming, not meditation. . . . As opposed to daydreaming wherein you let your mind wander, with meditation you focus your thoughts. You give your attention to the verse, phrase, word, or teaching of Scripture you have chosen. Instead of mental aimlessness, in meditation your mind is on a track—it's going somewhere; it has direction. The direction your mind takes is determined by the method of meditation you choose.[10]

Rather than emptying our minds, biblical meditation involves filling our minds with God's Word. This is the intentional chewing, tasting, and ruminating upon God's Word. Far from "swish and spit" meditation, it is "sit and steep." We need to steep the Word in the water of our soul so that we are flavored and colored by the Bible (Ps. 119:15, 16, 27, 97). Here are some ways we can do that.

Prioritize quality over quantity. It would be great for us to devour large portions of Scripture with great impact. However, most of us cannot do that effectively and consistently. So, instead, purpose to spend time with a smaller text, and ensure that it is getting in you and over you in a good way. You might consider reading and praying through a psalm rather than reading several chapters in another book.

Read the text aloud. I was surprised recently to learn that until the twentieth century most people did not read silently. Instead they read aloud, sometimes quietly and others more loudly. A friend of mine recalls hearing his dad read God's Word aloud and then pray out loud every morning while this friend was getting

---

10. Donald S. Whitney, *Spiritual Disciplines for the Christian Life* (Colorado Springs: NavPress, 1991), 56.

ready for school. I've tried this myself and found it quite helpful, because it engages another one of my senses.

Interrogate the passage. To interrogate just means to ask questions. Who wrote the passage? Why did he write it? What does this teach me about God and his character? What is the correct response to this truth about God? When you read in Matthew 5:45 about God caring for all people who oppose him, what does that teach you about God? In what ways does he do this? What attribute is on display here? Where else do I see this attribute in neon lights?

Make specific applications to your life. As you interrogate the text, you will think of specific personal areas that need to be addressed. Considering again the end of Matthew 5, what does God's care for all people, even those who do not love him, teach us about him? What implications does this have for how I am to treat other people? How do you view people who do not look and act like you? How do you feel about them? Do you have an unjustified hatred of people? Does it show? What areas do you need to repent of? What does repentance look like?

Ask and answer how this makes you treasure Christ. The need to treasure Christ is so often neglected. Like Jacob wrestling with the angel, do not leave the Word until you are blessed! Ask how it showcases the work of Christ. For example, if you are mistreating enemies or friends, do you see how Jesus treated his enemies? He died for them. He loved them. He gave everything for them. You and I were those enemies! Through Paul's description in Romans 5:6–11, I can see Jesus and all of his self-giving love on display for enemies like you and me. The fact that Jesus loves the unlovely and the unloving makes me love him—and others.

Take it with you. Find a verse (or verses) that grips your heart and write it out. In some way, put it on a sticky note or your hand or your phone or the fridge or wherever you will see it. Our church has a number of men who work in government facilities that do not allow electronics in and out of their workplace. So they write verses on note cards and carry them in their pockets. Between meetings or at lunch or other breaks, they can take out the notes and read them. They can pray through verses again and freshly apply them. This leads to greater marveling at God for his grace. It is a way of treasuring God's Word in your heart.

Bible reading is far too precious a time to just go through the motions. You must get that Word into your heart, mind, and life. This takes work. So resolve today to not practice the "swish and spit" dental-chair devotional life. Instead prayerfully soak in the text, interrogate it, and take it with you.

Prayer

Oftentimes Christians struggle with prayer because they forget the wonderful intimacy that comes from their relationship with God. We forget the access and we forget his love.

Jesus taught us to call God our Father (Matt. 6:9), and the Holy Spirit compels our hearts to cry out to God, calling him Father (Rom. 8:14–17). This new relationship of being God's child brings a new heart cry. It is the cry of intimacy, expectation, familiarity, and love.

Recently one of my children brought me one of her running shoes. The laces were in several knots. She had obviously attempted to untie a knot herself but had only added more knots to the equation. Finally, after realizing she was outmatched, she brought the sneaker to me and asked, "Daddy, can you untie this?"

Prayer is much like this. We come to our heavenly Father with our hearts and lives all tied up in impossible knots. Our own efforts to remove the problems only compound them. So we turn to him in prayer and ask, "Father, can you untangle this?" He is your Father, so he delights to hear your requests. He delights to attend your greatest burdens, anxieties, needs, and fears with his mercy, grace, love, and generosity. He is your Father; he delights to untie the knots of your heart.

It is this reminder that God is not only able but also willing to work in our lives that drives us to pray. He is the true and greater Father who would never ignore or turn away his children. He welcomes you to himself. We are to wear out a path to that throne of grace to free our hearts from the snarl of discontentment. We come to him confessing our personal weakness, temptations, sins, and fears. He hears and he answers. Even earthly fathers hear and answer their children; how much more our heavenly Father who commands us to pray.

How Should We Pray?

But how should we pray? I appreciate John Calvin's rules of prayer to help in this pursuit.[11] Before offering his guidelines, he reminds us of the benefit of fixing certain times for prayer. If we don't schedule times, Calvin warns, prayer will slip from our memory, and we will be distracted by other things.

First, have a heartfelt sense of reverence for God. While we have confident access to God (Heb. 4:16), we do not come to him flippantly or irreverently. Our minds and hearts are to be aware of the One we are speaking to. When we are reminded of God's majesty, we are graciously freed from many of the earthly cares and afflictions that weigh us down and distract us.

Second, have a heartfelt sense of personal need and repentance. We must come to God as beggars, says Calvin. Anything we have comes from him, and everything that he gives is subject to his all-wise will. Keeping his glory in focus, we are trained to approach him in repentance from sin and in subjection to his will.

Third, have a heartfelt sense of humility and trust in God. When we are really praying, then we have abandoned all confidence in ourselves and are humbly pleading for his gracious pardon. If we approach God in any other way, we will come as those pridefully presuming upon him, relegating him to service as our

---

11. Joel R. Beeke, "The Communion of Men with God," in *John Calvin: A Heart for Devotion, Doctrine, Doxology*, ed. Burk Parsons (Lake Mary, FL: Reformation Trust, 2008), 236–37.

butler. We pray to God because he is *God* and we need his loving care.

Fourth, have a heartfelt sense of confident hope. The basis for answered prayer is neither our goodness nor our skill in prayer. Instead, it is God's grace, kindness, and love. Any success in our praying comes from the successful work of Christ, "for the blood of our Lord Jesus Christ seals the pact which God has concluded with us."[12] Our boldness in prayer is based upon God welcoming us to the throne on the merit of Christ (Heb. 4:14–16).

Sensing that this might seem out of reach for laymen who want to be faithful in prayer, Calvin helped to put it in perspective, as Joel Beeke explains:

> These rules may seem overwhelming—even unattainable—in the face of a holy, omniscient God. Calvin acknowledges that our prayers are fraught with weakness and failure. "No one has ever carried this out with the uprightness that was due," he writes. But God tolerates "even our stammering and pardons our ignorance," allowing us to gain familiarity with Him in prayer, though it be in "a babbling manner." In short, we will never feel like worthy petitioners. Our checkered prayer life is often attacked by doubts, but such struggles show us our ongoing need for prayer itself as a "lifting up of the spirit" and continually drive us to Jesus Christ, who alone will "change the throne of dreadful glory into the throne of grace." Calvin concludes that "Christ is the only way, and the one access, by which it is granted us to come to God."[13]

A Sample Day

In addition to Calvin, I have found many other authors and teachers to be helpful in this pursuit. Recently Tim Keller surveyed the prayer practices of Augustine, Martin Luther, and John Calvin.

12. Wilhelm Niesel, *The Theology of Calvin* (Philadelphia: Westminster Press, 1956), 156.
13. Beeke, "The Communion of Men with God," 237.

Keller's *Prayer: Experiencing Awe and Intimacy with God*[14] is eminently practical and I highly recommend it. In the following outline, I have applied many of Keller's suggestions and principles while taking Calvin's advice to be sure to schedule prayer. In view of contentment, this plan helps me to resist dental-chair devotions and continues to scrub my heart for idols that foster discontentment.

"Pregame" (early morning—45 minutes)
1. Wake up.
2. Pray and ask for illumination (Piper's IOUS is very helpful here).
3. Read a chapter or two of the Bible from a reading plan.
4. Read, pray, and meditate through a psalm.
   a. Write down in a journal key themes or terms that are particularly striking.
   b. Prayerfully interact with the text.
   c. Begin writing out some structure and themes.
   d. Summarize the section.
   e. Find a key verse (or two) that is particularly arresting.
   f. Turn this verse into the scaffolding for my prayer.
   g. Write down more theological and practical implications of the passage.
   h. Pray through these notes for myself and others.

"Halftime" (midday—10 minutes)
1. Recall particular verses and implications from the morning (rereading if necessary).
2. Take inventory of my heart to see if particular vices, besetting sins, or other idols are crowding out my love for Christ.

---

14. New York: Dutton, 2014.

3. Clear accounts through confession and repentance.
4. Recall others who need prayer at this time.
5. Pray for faithfulness throughout the afternoon and evening.

"Postgame" (evening—15 minutes)
1. Read through another psalm, perhaps with less detailed interaction than in the morning but using some of the same principles of thoughtful meditation.
2. Review the day, confessing sin and clinging to Christ's merit.
3. Consider praying with my spouse.
4. Pray for needs that have surfaced through the day.
5. Give thanks for particular blessings enjoyed.
6. Be reminded of how God has sustained me with his bread this day.

▬ ▬ ▬

It is a self-evident truth that those who persist in the spiritual disciplines grow in grace, and those who don't persist, don't grow. I have never met a mature believer who is not faithful in private devotions. Like the cumulative, compounding effect of military training, the daily work of prayer, Bible reading, and meditation will shape us more and more into the likeness of Christ. And when we are thinking in terms of contentment, this likeness is the mark we are after, because Christ remains the most content man who ever lived.

Review Questions

1. What is the main point of the Christian life?

2. What is the main difference between what Paul's contemporaries taught and what he taught about contentment?

3. Where do we most often look for contentment today?

4. What does our lack of attention to spiritual disciplines reveal about what we believe about contentment?

5. What changes can you make in your life to prioritize learning contentment?

5

See Through the Shiny Wrappers

When the Serpent approached Eve in the garden of Eden, he found a woman who was content. She had never felt the wandering thoughts of something better, because she rested in the One who was best. The person, promises, and provision of God were sufficient to satisfy her.

But the Serpent was crafty. How did he display his craftiness? It was through his cunning and deceitful charm that he began to lure Eve away. He packaged his lies in such a way that they looked like truth. He made choosing death seem like such an appealing decision that Eve actually thought it would make her happy.

We see his tactics when we read in Genesis 3:1 that Satan attacked God's word: "Did God actually say . . . ?" First Satan attacked the clarity of God's word, implying that God's word could not be known. Then he attacked God's truthfulness: "You will not surely die." By attacking the truthfulness of God's word, Satan was saying that God himself cannot be trusted. And finally, he attacked God's motive: "God knows that when you eat it you will be like God, knowing good and evil." Satan suggested that God had bad intentions; he was keeping something from her. The fork-tongued liar invited Eve to judge God's Word and God's character. For the first time in the history of the world, God was being scrutinized.

But the Evil One did not stop there. Sensing that his trophy was within reach, he encouraged Eve to assess the fruit on the forbidden tree. She began to evaluate it and convinced herself to eat it. Seeing that it was "good for food, and that it was a delight to the eyes, and that the tree was to be desired to make one wise, she took of its fruit and ate, and she gave some to her husband, who was with her, and he ate" (Gen. 3:6).

Here we are confronted with the plan of Satan to belittle God's glory by luring people into sin. He tempted her and she fell. The shocking detail that we often forget about this passage is that Adam and Eve did not want for anything! It wasn't like they were starving; the entire world, but for one tree, was their pantry. They weren't lacking beautiful surroundings; every scene was a glorious landscape of visual delight. And they truly had wisdom, for they feared and obeyed God (Prov. 9:10). But, for the first time ever, God's human creations strayed from God's lap, where they had previously sat like children embraced by their welcoming father, and they wandered away into the realm of wanting.

Satan had deceptively packaged death in a shiny wrapper and sold it as life. And the crafty Serpent prevailed. He seized upon an opportunity to unfasten our first parents' dependence on God. There was first a breach, and then he opened it wide. Adam and Eve turned away from God and his word, seeking to be satisfied in creation rather than God, their Creator (Rom. 1:25). This is what it means to be discontent. Satan came with his slick promises to give them something they did not need. But instead of meeting any needs, he led them away from God, who alone can meet their needs.

This is Satan's agenda. It has not changed much since Eden. He is as tireless as ever, dangling the false promises in shiny wrappers before men, women, and children and watching them take and eat.

As we know, the story goes on. Adam—previously silent, even while standing by—also ate the fruit. By this disobedience to God, Adam and all humanity after him now came under the curse of sin. Yet God pursued the shamed couple. He came to them with the gracious words of a God who is both Savior and Judge. He made clothes to cover them and then announced a curse upon the Serpent, the people, and the rest of creation. The indication is that this altercation between our first parents and the Serpent was simply round one in an ongoing struggle with sin and its consequences. There would be many more days of difficulty ahead.

Life now would be much harder. There would be tears, death, guilt, and shame. The Serpent would be active amid this new, dark, and drastically different world. So God ushered the couple out of the garden to go and face this new world together, but not alone. He went with them, speaking words of truth with his promise of rest and restoration abiding over them. But now, as they went, they would carry the memory of what they had before, like a shadow over their present experiences. They would hunger to be back in Eden and have their souls satisfied in God alone.

In the meantime, humanity would have to deal with the god of this world. Whether young or old, all of the sons and daughters of Adam and Eve would be faced with the shiny wrappers of temptation.

Recently my young daughter was captivated by what appeared to be junk in nice ·wrapping paper. My wife had gone to a fabric store to get a few items when our six-year-old saw a box covered with a picture of "Elsa," plenty of snowflakes, glitter, and all the requisite sparkles to get her attention. She ran up to the box and announced with all the urgency she could muster, "I need this." As my wife took a look at it, she had to laugh. Beyond the glitter and sparkles there was a small plastic curling iron, a blow-dryer the size of her hand, and tiny plastic hair rollers. The price tag for this plastic replica of beauty supplies was twenty-five dollars.

Zoë didn't go to the store with Mom considering a purchase of model hair dryers, but when she saw Elsa and the sparkles, lust was conceived. Her desire to be like her two older sisters was aroused at the sight of that glistening box. Can you imagine what her reaction would have been if my wife had bought her that nonworking toy? Perhaps you have seen the look on a child's face when she realized a toy she wanted did not live up to expectations. Perhaps you yourself have experienced the letdown of discovering that something you desired did not match the hype. Yes, as the children of Adam and Eve, we like our shiny wrappers.

The God of This World

We live in the midst of a world that is not what it once was and with hearts craving to be back in Eden. Meanwhile, we are reminded by preachers that we are not to love the world. But preachers (and others) have to be careful, thoughtful, and clear when they say things like this.

In Wendell Berry's book *Jayber Crow*,[1] Jayber is the town barber. He goes to Sunday service because he likes the company of the women at church, but he despises hypocrisy in the preaching. He repines over the weekly prattling about how we should hate the world. Jayber finds it ironic that, after service, the preacher enjoys several helpings for lunch. Surely, Jayber thinks, this preacher's hatred for the world is a bit inconsistent, as it does not extend to "all things" involving biscuits and chicken!

So, what does the Bible mean by the word *world*? There are a number of different ways to answer this question. A particular passage may use the word *world* to refer to all the people living. Sometimes it refers specifically to non-Jewish people. Other times, *world* may refer to all of the geographic space on the planet. Still other times, it refers to the entire universe.

But there is another sense in which the word *world* is used.

---

1. Wendell Berry, *Jayber Crow* (Washington, DC: Counterpoint, 2000), 160–61.

Often when the Bible speaks negatively about the world (e.g., "Do not love the world," 1 John 2:15) it is referring to the world system. Scripture tells us that Satan is the god of this world (2 Cor. 4:4) and therefore the commander in the global rebellion. Let's not forget that ultimately this undercurrent of rebellion is against God. It is a religious system of opposition to the true God, and it exists with the mission statement of belittling God's glory through the promotion of lawlessness.

When we hear of a tragedy and act of terror, we may briefly comfort ourselves with the fact that the incident took place far away. However, while terrorism may strive to topple governments, we need to understand the sense in which Satan is the government. As we've observed, he is referred to as the god of this world (2 Cor. 4:4; Eph. 2:1–3). This entire world, in this sense, is under the rule and sway of the Evil One. As Christians we do not despair of this fact because we understand that even in his malevolence Satan cannot operate without the expressed permission of our good and sovereign God. As in the story of Job, he cannot move without sanction from heaven. This truth, however, does not diminish the fact confirmed by Scripture and experience that the world itself is bent against God.

With this ruler, the world system is committed to sin. This is another way of saying the world system is committed to making you discontent. As Matt Smethurst put it, "The world, the flesh and the Devil have a Great Commission of their own—to stir up discontentment and lure us away from the gospel."[2]

What's the Battle Plan?

When I talk about a worldwide battle and a demonic agenda to stir up discontentment, your eyebrows may rise up in protest. "Isn't this a bit extreme? When I think of battle scenes I think

---

2. Matt Smethurst, "Contentment Does Not Come Naturally," *TGC* (*The Gospel Coalition*), October 16, 2014, http://www.thegospelcoalition.org/article/contentment-does-not-come-naturally.

of carnage, pain, death, and despair. This seems like a bit of an overstatement."

But, this demonic agenda is precisely the type of deception that is afoot. We don't often realize the influence upon us and this world. It is important to remember that we live amid an undercurrent that is godless and god-opposed. It is not neutral. And so it must be resisted.

When you go to the beach, you quickly become aware of the current in the ocean. Simply wading in the surf, you can feel it pull at your feet as the waves wash in and out, pulling away the very sand you are standing on. If you go out twenty or thirty feet from the shore, you can feel that current in a whole other way. As you attempt to stay upright amid the waves, you can feel the current against your legs and back. And before long, you look back at your things on the shore and notice that you have moved. The current has subtly and imperceptibly pulled you down the shoreline, away from where you started.

In this world, we have to understand that we are not standing on the pavement or even the dry sand of the beach—we are actually in the water. A strong undercurrent pulls us. If we are not paying attention, we will be moved off-center and drift dangerously away. The mission of those who oppose God is to belittle his glory by disobeying his rule and convincing us to do likewise. One of the chief expressions of this disobedience comes when, like Adam and Eve, we are not content in God. In order to learn contentment, we must be able to see, assess, and discern things biblically. To do this, we need to know the battle plan and how it is executed.

How Is the Battle Plan Executed?

If you were Satan, how would you labor to make people discontent? You would have to get them to distrust God as the one who can truly meet their needs. And then you would have to build their hopes to find happiness, purpose, identity, and satisfaction in things that cannot bear the freight of humanity's need. If contentment is learned by resting in what we cannot see, discontentment results from seeking rest in physical things. The Evil One's tactic appeals to our desire to assess the benefit of something by what we see. It appeals to our own perception of need and desire for pleasure. This was the tactical plan of Genesis 3, and it is the ongoing plan today. Remember, Eve saw that the fruit was a delight to her eyes (Gen. 3:6). Satan hasn't needed to contrive a new tactical plan; the old one is working just fine.

C. S. Lewis's *Screwtape Letters* is an extended dialogue between Screwtape, a senior demon, and his young nephew Wormwood, a junior tempter. Screwtape is passing on advice for ruining people; or, we might say, making them discontent:

> Never forget that when we are dealing with any pleasure in its healthy and normal and satisfying form, we are, in a sense, on the Enemy's [i.e., God's] ground. I know we have won many a soul through pleasure. All the same, it is his invention, not ours. He made the pleasures: all our research so far has not enabled us to produce one. All we can do is to encourage the humans to take the pleasures which our Enemy has produced, at times, or in ways, or in degrees, which He has forbidden. . . . There are things for humans to do all day long without His minding in the least—sleeping, washing, eating, drinking, making love, playing, praying, working. Everything has to be twisted before it's any use to us.[3]

This work of twisting and alluring is called temptation. However, when we talk about temptation, there is often confusion about where the temptation comes from. Is it from people and things or is it from within?

I have found John Owen to be very helpful in pinning down a definition of temptation and its source.

> A temptation, then, in general is anything that, for any reason, exerts a force or influence to seduce and draw the mind and

---

3. C. S. Lewis, *The Screwtape Letters* (San Francisco: HarperSanFrancisco, 2001), 44.

heart of man from the obedience which God requires of him to any kind of sin.

In particular, it is a temptation if it causes a man to sin, gives him opportunity to do so, or causes him to neglect his duty.

Using language that represents Satan's overarching strategy for promoting disobedience, Owen shows us that the battleground is in the heart and mind. This is where the work is done. How does it work? Owen goes on: "Temptation may suggest evil to the heart, or draw out the evil that is already there. It is also a temptation to a man if something is by any means able to distract him from his communion with God, or the consistent universal obedience that is required of him."[4]

Temptation draws us away from obedience to God. This is another way of saying temptation is about drawing us away from worshiping God. And if the heart of worship is rejoicing in God's matchless worth, temptation draws the heart into discontentment. You can see the deceptive fingerprints of the Serpent here. Temptation aims to make us discontent in God by flirtatiously luring us to pursue contentment in created things instead of the Creator (Rom. 1:25). We are thereby tempted away from the only true source of contentment. This vicious cycle only gets worse and our condition more and more bleak as the heart is trained to turn away from God. The result is a heart that is locked in the dungeon of discontentment.

This is basically what we read in the first chapter of James:

Let no one say when he is tempted, "I am being tempted by God," for God cannot be tempted with evil, and he himself tempts no one. But each person is tempted when he is lured and enticed by his own desire. Then desire when it has conceived gives birth to sin, and sin when it is fully grown brings forth death. (1:13–15)

---

4. John Owen, *Temptation: Resisted and Repulsed*, ed. Richard Rushing (Carlisle, PA: Banner of Truth, 2007), 10.

Notice that it is not God who tempts us, but we are tempted from within. Our desires or lusts lure and entice us. James uses picturesque language to make this point. The word translated "lured" is a hunting term used of luring an animal into a trap. The trap is baited and the animal is lured in. The term translated "enticed" is a fishing term that describes catching a fish with bait. But notice how the luring and enticing actually work: "Each person is tempted when he is lured and enticed by his own desire." It is our desire or our lust that makes the bait look good. We want something. We feel like we need something. We crave something, and so we are susceptible to temptation.

We saw in Genesis 3 that Eve's heart desired something. She was tempted by a promise of more. She lusted after the shiny wrappers that falsely promised life, satisfaction, and liberty. But like cheap holiday candy in slick packaging, the thing so much hyped and so much desired sorely disappointed. False promises only leave us wanting more. They cannot deliver.

One day I was driving down the interstate with my family. We passed a billboard that read, "Granite—on sale!" It boasted thirty-nine square feet of it. My wife exclaimed, "Baby! Did you see that?" After a few minutes of dialogue, we moved on to another topic. But the bait had been taken, and Christie's heart had latched onto the idea of new countertops. Over the next day or two she had to wrestle through whether we needed new countertops at all. It was a sanctifying trial.

In that instance we both rode by the same sign but had different reactions. The bait and the hook were laid out before us. But it was my wife's desire that latched onto it. In another instance, I might have been the one tempted; but this time it was her turn. The sign was tempting— but her desire made it so. This is the way temptations work. They are personal rather than universal. Each heart is filled with desires and has its own vulnerabilities. What is universal is the desire to be content, and so we are lured and enticed by created things, though not necessarily the same things.

Owen provides some timeless examples:

> To clarify, I am considering temptation not just as the active force of seduction to sin, but also the thing itself by which we are tempted. Whatever it is, within us or without us, that hinders us from duty or provides an occasion for sin, this should be considered temptation. It could be business, employment, the course of one's life, company affections, nature, corrupt purposes, relations, delights, reputation, esteem, position, abilities, gifts, etc., that provide the opportunity to sin or neglect duty. These are true temptations just as much as the most violent solicitations of Satan or allurements of the world. Whoever does not realize this is on the brink of ruin.[5]

Temptation's Lures

In 1 John we read of some very helpful categories for considering temptation. As you will see, they correspond well with what our first parents faced. We may call these categories lures. Satan fishes these lures in discontented hearts to draw them or keep them from God. The apostle John alerts us to these lures to help us better understand the battle for contentment. He does not want us to be enticed by colorful decoys or shiny wrappers. Instead, he wants us to rest in the sufficiency of God and find ourselves satisfied in him alone.

John writes, "For all that is in the world—the desires of the flesh and the desires of the eyes and pride of life—is not from the Father but is from the world" (1 John 2:16).

Lure 1: The Desires of the Flesh

John first warns us of the "the desires of the flesh." The Greek word translated "desires" here (*epithymia*) could also be translated "lusts." When we say "lust," we automatically think in negative terms. However, the Greek word is neutral. Whether a desire

---

5. Ibid., 10–11.

is good or bad depends on the goodness and appropriateness of what it fixes itself on. Consider these two examples: "If anyone aspires to the office of overseer, he desires a noble task." Here in 1 Timothy 3:1, the word is used for a man's good and noble desire for the office of elder. Now hear the same word used in Matthew's Gospel: "Everyone who looks at a woman with lustful intent has already committed adultery with her in his heart" (Matt. 5:28). Obviously here the desire is inappropriate; the woman in view is not the man's wife. It is sinful for him to desire or lust after her. Not every craving or desire is sinful in itself; however, when cravings are pursued at the expense of God's glory or contrary to his Word, they are sinful.

In 1 John 2:16, "the desires of the flesh" are the cravings of a fallen human nature that seeks to live independently from God and find satisfaction in created things. The flesh is considered the seat of opposition to God within our fallen nature. We see how the desires of the flesh give birth to the works of the flesh in Galatians 5:

> Now the works of the flesh are evident: sexual immorality, impurity, sensuality, idolatry, sorcery, enmity, strife, jealousy, fits of anger, rivalries, dissensions, divisions, envy, drunkenness, orgies, and things like these. I warn you, as I warned you before, that those who do such things will not inherit the kingdom of God. (5:19–21)

The Scriptures are showing us that worldliness expresses itself through the desire of the flesh, which craves self-fulfillment independently of God. This is the default human condition since we were banished from the garden of Eden. The apostle Paul offers this summary in Ephesians 2:

> And you were dead in the trespasses and sins in which you once walked, following the course of this world, following the prince of the power of the air, the spirit that is now at work in the sons of disobedience—among whom we all once lived in the passions of our flesh, carrying out the desires of the body

and the mind, and were by nature children of wrath, like the rest of mankind. (Eph. 2:1–3)

Notice how Paul shows that prior to conversion it is the norm to live in the "passions" (the noun form of the same word translated "lust," "desire") of our flesh. But mark this key point: this only happens when you believe you do not have what you need. If we are truly content in God, the lust of the flesh is stymied. But if, like Adam and Eve, we fail to believe God's promises, rejoice in God's provision, and delight in God's person, we too will be trapped in the vicious cycle of discontentment.

Lure 2: The Desires of the Eyes

Next, John warns us of "the desires of the eyes." This expression could mean either the way we look at things or what we look at. In other words, we are lured into desiring good things we see, yet in a wrong way, or looking at sinful things. The eyes of the soul become fixed on created things as the means to fulfillment and purpose. Think of Esau. He gave up his blessing for a bowl of soup (Gen. 25:29–35). He saw something he wanted, and he was willing to sacrifice anything for it. What he saw became the consuming passion of the moment, and he forfeited God's blessing to him.

This reminds us that contentment is inward and spiritual. It comes to us by grace. To attempt to fill a void in the soul with created things is futile.

We are instructed in the tenth commandment not to covet. But when our eyes latch onto what others have, we become discontent with what we've been given by God and jealously desire more. To obey the tenth commandment is to be content, even rejoicing in what God has graciously given us.

In a particular podcast, women voiced struggles with Facebook because they always see there other women's perfectly decorated homes, wonderful vacations, perfect selfies, and happy families.

"Why can't I have that?" said one of the women, admitting the effect of this filtered view of friends' lives. The heart craves what the eyes see. Too often men look for comfort, happiness, and joy by turning their eyes to pornography. A natural (and good) desire for a woman is twisted into coveting what is outside what God has sanctioned as good. Seeking to satisfy their discontentment with images, they feed the cravings of the heart through the eyes.

Our hearts are deceptive, untrustworthy guides (Jer. 17:9). And even our natural vision can deceive us. Years ago I was training for a marathon. Running so many miles meant that I was almost constantly eating. In the middle of the night I would awake with intense hunger. I'd make my way down to the kitchen and look for something to eat. One night I worked through some ham and cheese, then reached for something to quench my thirst. I grabbed the bowl of what looked to me like pineapple juice and lifted it to my face to enjoy a sweet punctuation to my midnight snack. The only trouble was, it was not pineapple juice. It was liquid egg whites! It took me a few gulps to realize this, and my chalky mouth reminded me that things are not always as they appear. Like other temptations, the bowl did not deliver on its promise. If I cannot always trust my eyes, neither can I trust my heart to evaluate things apart from God's Word and Spirit.

Shiny wrappers catch the eye, but our souls are fed not by what is seen and perishing (1 John 2:17) but by what is unseen and eternal (2 Cor. 4:18). We thwart the schemes of the Enemy when we remember that the path to contentment is not through the physical and external but through what is spiritual and internal.

Lure 3: The Pride of Possessions

The final lure we are warned of is the "pride of life." While the first two have to do with desires for things, this one has to do with pride in what you already have. The NASB translates this phrase in 1 John 2:16 as "the boastful pride of life." It is a pride rooted in who we think we are as measured by what we possess or have accomplished. In the context of this verse, such pride is baseless.

Surely you have felt this type of lure. We all struggle to some degree with boasting in ourselves and taking pride in things we've done. Many people are oblivious to their own boasting. Have you ever met a professional bragger, what comedian Brian Regan calls the "Me-Monster"? This is the obnoxious person who trips over himself to talk about who he is and what he's done. No matter what you say, the Me-Monster one-ups you with a story of his supremacy. Every sentence is a chance to showcase his pride.

The Me-Monster may seem content with himself, but actually he's not. His clamoring for attention is a cry for legitimacy and acceptance. In other words, he's discontent. That's because a contented spirit is a quiet spirit. It is resting. It does not need to clamor for affirmation, validation, or amazement. A content person is able to sit quietly under the reassuring affirmation of God. The Lord is his or her sufficiency.

The Expiration Date

Not only do false promises in shiny wrappers not deliver, but the whole world system that manufactures them is doomed. John goes on to show that the world and its system have an expiration date. "The world is passing away along with its desires, but whoever does the will of God abides forever" (1 John 2:17). The implication here is clear: it is foolish to love the world. The seeds of death are embedded deep in the produce of the world. Don't eat its rotten fruit.

The tactics of the god of this world only work on one who is discontent. Satan is the god of this world, the fierce opponent to God, his glory, and his people. In the evil one's effort to promote disobedience, he perverts the good gifts of God and tempts people to find ultimate meaning in them. God, however, pulls back the curtain and exposes it all. He shows the futility and foolishness of taking the bait. And he provides a better way forward.

Collapsing upon the God Who Abides Forever

John provides a contrast that is compelling and stark: "The world is passing away along with its desires, but whoever does the will of God abides forever" (1 John 2:17). This contrast goes alongside verse 15, which pits loving the world against loving the Father: "Do not love the world or the things in the world. If anyone loves the world, the love of the Father is not in him" (1 John 2:15). Here is the true answer to the wayward desires of the human heart: collapse upon the God who abides forever! In the midst of the change, decay, discouragement, and pain in this world, John opens the windows to the cross-breeze of heaven. The air of grace refreshes our hearts.

John shows us that the natural impulse of the fallen nature is to crave self at the expense of God, while the new nature craves God as the fulfillment of self. Such is the gracious distinction between the lures of the world and the will of God.

- - -

Discontentment comes from believing false promises. Like a subtle current at our feet, the world system opposes us wave after wave. The god of this world has been on his destructive mission since the garden of Eden marketing phony "saviors" in shiny wrappers. Learning contentment is learning to see through the shiny wrappers and assess these temptations with discernment. Those who do so will find themselves more and more content in God, satisfied in his unmatched and unfading sufficiency.

Review Questions

1. Summarize what Satan's tactical plan was with Adam and Eve in the garden.

2. What is the connection between God, his Word, and our contentment?

3. In your own words, what is temptation?

4. What are the three lures listed in 1 John? Which of these three strikes you as the most persistent in your life?

5. When evaluating temptation, what promises must you believe in order to see through the shiny wrappers?

6

Just Say No!

In 1982, then First Lady Nancy Reagan was speaking to school-children in Oakland about staying drug free. One of the children raised her hand and asked Mrs. Reagan what to do if someone offered her drugs. The First Lady said, "Well, you just say no." Reagan's unscripted reply became the tagline for the nation's antidrug campaign. The genius of the slogan "Just say no" lies in its simplicity. Everyone can remember these three simple words. But more than this, everyone can remember why these three simple words matter. Drug use will destroy your life. In morbid irony, rarely does anyone begin using drugs to destroy his or her life. It's the exact opposite; people begin using drugs because they are mired in unhappiness, pain, and discontentment—and want a way out.

When we think from a biblical worldview, we understand that drugs are so dangerous because they are used to bring something that only God can bring. We know that true and abiding happiness can only be found in a right relationship with him. However, by craving things apart from him, we put ourselves in all types of trouble.

The heart of the matter is that when we ourselves determine

what will satisfy, we don't pursue what brings true satisfaction. The broken compass within us always leads to the dumpster rather than the five-star restaurant. We are painfully off in our calibration. The problem is not that we are seeking satisfaction; it's the way we naturally seek it. To find true satisfaction, we have to "just say no" to ourselves. Or, to put it biblically, we must deny ourselves.

As Christians we understand that self-denial is not an impossible ideal; it's a practical necessity. Jesus essentially carved it into the doorframe of the church: "And he said to all, 'If anyone would come after me, let him deny himself and take up his cross daily and follow me'" (Luke 9:23). If we are to walk over the threshold and join Christ's other followers, we must deny ourselves.

This should make total sense to us as we think about our need for contentment and where to find it. Throughout this book I have been contending that all sin is tied to the first sin in the garden. At its core, sin is an expression of discontentment with our Creator. Instead of receiving and rejoicing in God as the greatest gift, we foolishly pursue our contentment in created things (cf. Rom. 1:18–25). When Jesus comes to bring us back to God (1 Pet. 3:18), he saves us in large part from ourselves. Like a child playing with matches, an addict with needles, or a wealthy man with his greed, we don't know how to say no to ourselves. We keep gorging ourselves on stuff that we think will satisfy us, but it only makes things worse. Little wonder, then, that Jesus says with such clarity to anyone who would even consider following him, "Let him deny himself."

We should also remember that self-denial is not simply the posture we take as we cross the threshold into conversion. It is the posture and pursuit of the entire Christian life. Like humility, self-denial is something most people can talk about vaguely but not explain in detail. Since it is so critical to our pursuit of contentment, I want to spend some time thinking through it in detail. We will consider its reorientation, repudiation, and reception.

A Reorientation

Self-denial is not natural. We naturally love ourselves. I have been in counseling situations where I've explained what the Bible says in what seemed to be biblical straight talk, only to be surprised to hear, in reply, "I agree. I need to love people more, but first I need to learn to love myself." The influence of the self-help industry and the prophets of self-esteem is truly far-reaching. The concept of loving ourselves is the prevailing cultural framework. We are not that bad; we deserve better; and we can get there if we try harder. A strong cultural wind batters us with this emphasis. Even as Christians we might not realize its impact on us, but it is there.

One of my favorite childhood memories is of a trip to see the "Old Man of the Mountain" in New Hampshire.[1] Over a period of many, many years the side of the mountain had been carved by the elements into the striking resemblance of an old man's face.

As we live amid a world with strong cultural forces, we too are being shaped and molded. Therefore, it is important that we as Christians build our understanding on something more sure, something that will not erode or collapse. As followers of Jesus we must reorient our identities and pursuits around the Word of God. And there we find Jesus's revolutionary words, "If anyone would come after me, let him deny himself and take up his cross and follow me" (Matt. 16:24; Mark 8:34; Luke 9:23).

A Repudiation

Let's think a bit about what denying ourselves actually is. The word translated "deny" means disown or disassociate.[2] It was used of Peter when, under pressure, he publicly disassociated himself from Christ:

> Now Peter was sitting outside in the courtyard. And a servant girl came up to him and said, "You also were with Jesus the

---

1. Sadly, in 2003 the natural sculpture of the "Old Man of the Mountain" collapsed.
2. "Deny," in *Holman Illustrated Bible Dictionary*, rev. ed., ed. Chad Brand et al. (Nashville: Holman, 2003), 413.

Galilean." But he denied it before them all, saying, "I do not know what you mean." And when he went out to the entrance, another servant girl saw him, and she said to the bystanders, "This man was with Jesus of Nazareth." And again he denied it with an oath: "I do not know the man." (Matt. 26:69–72)

So what does Jesus mean when he says that all who would follow him must deny themselves? He means that we need to repudiate or reject everything we have previously built our lives on. This mandates a rejection of a life based on self-interest and self-fulfillment.[3] The follower of Jesus must deny *himself*, not just his sins; he cannot be self-centered.[4] Peter foolishly attempted to gain his life by denying his association with Christ, but we are to deny ourselves so that we may gain Christ.

While this idea is simple enough to grasp, it remains hard to master in practice. But if we are going to chase contentment, then we must learn the hard lessons of self-denial. It is among the basic disciplines of Christianity. Think of how much work it takes to teach children the alphabet, pronunciation, and how to read. It is difficult but important work. One of the incentives that keep teachers persevering is the long-term value of mastering these foundational lessons. Children may, in time, ascend to very successful careers, but they will never move beyond the basics of reading, writing, and communication. It is the same with the lessons of self-denial; if we are to make any real progress in this business of contentment, we must master the ABC's of denying ourselves.[5]

We can be thankful that self-denial is something God is committed to teaching us. He commands it upon our entry into his

3. Robert H. Stein, *Luke*, The New American Commentary 24 (Nashville: Broadman & Holman, 1992), 279.

4. Leon Morris, *Luke: An Introduction and Commentary*, Tyndale New Testament Commentaries 3 (Downers Grove, IL: InterVarsity Press, 1988), 188–89.

5. Jeremiah, Burroughs, *The Rare Jewel of Christian Contentment* (Edinburgh: Banner of Truth, 1979), 87.

family, and it is an ongoing priority as we move forward. If you have made some progress in this area, you will no doubt have noticed that it softens your heart. To illustrate this, Jeremiah Burroughs observed that when you hit something soft, it doesn't make a noise, but when you hit something that's hard, it does. Our hearts are naturally so full of ourselves, and as a result hardened by self-love, that when we encounter any difficulty, we tend to make noise by grumbling and complaining. But if we are denying ourselves, we are more apt to yield to God's hand quietly—even in the difficulty. Burroughs writes, "When you strike a woolsack it makes no noise because it yields to the stroke; so a self-denying heart yields to the stroke and thereby comes to this contentment."[6]

What do we need to know and believe in order to come to this place of quiet self-denial? To answer this, I want to interact with a number of observations from Burroughs that I find immensely helpful in the pursuit of contentment. These expressions serve as personal reminders to deny ourselves.

"I Am Nothing"

To say that "I am nothing" does not conflict with the biblical teaching of the dignity of human life. We are made in the image of God and given wonderful blessings and privileges. What's more, we even do some relative good to one another and God's creation. However, I am speaking here of ultimate good. The Bible makes clear that there is no one who does good, not even one (Rom. 3:12). In the most important sense, we have missed the point of life. Instead of loving God and enjoying his creation, we have sinned and perverted his good gifts. To say that we are nothing means that we have nothing of ultimate value or goodness in ourselves. The psalmist got this exactly right when he exclaimed,

You are my Lord;
I have no good apart from you. (Ps. 16:2)

---
6. Ibid.

Certainly you can see the immediate practicality of this. The person who knows that she is nothing is able to bear anything. Does this sound contradictory? I assure you it is not. Once we realize our utter emptiness, we can actually seek help from outside ourselves. So much of our problem is seeking to find something from within, but the cupboard is bear.

Isn't this what makes God's pursuit of us in the gospel so refreshing? He pursues and arrests us by his grace. Though it may seem severe to think you are nothing, in the gospel you have Christ to be your everything! Everything you need is found in him. The pursuit of contentment requires the repudiation of self. The psalmist knew this and cried out to God,

> Preserve me, O God, for in you I take refuge.
> I say to the LORD, "You are my Lord;
>   I have no good apart from you." (Ps. 16:1–2)

"I Deserve Nothing"

One day, our family picked up some fast food at a local burger franchise. It had been a long day, the kids were tired, and they needed to eat. Because I was "trying" to be healthy, I didn't order anything and just joined the kids at the table while my wife fixed something with kale and hemp in it. After giving thanks for the food, I reached over to my three-year-old son's fries and grabbed one. As I stuffed it in my mouth, he said, "Daaaad! That's my French fry!" And technically he was right. It was his. I had given it to him. It was my responsibility to feed him.

But with our heavenly Father, we are like children who ran away from home. We gave up our birthright. We forsook his provision and deserve nothing good. This has strong implications for how we view God's provisions for us, as well as his provisions for others in comparison.

Say we come to notice something that someone else has and we want. In other words, we start to covet. Secretly within our hearts we envy our neighbor and become resentful toward God for not giving this desired possession to us. You can imagine how remembering that we deserve nothing except hell would change things, whether in the home, the neighborhood, the workplace, or the church. Yet we complain against God when we forget what we truly deserve and what we have been graciously given. Remembering that we are nothing and that we deserve nothing will help us deny ourselves.

"I Can Do Nothing"

Jesus reminds us that apart from him we can do nothing (John 15:5). This is where the reality of following Jesus comes into direct conflict with popular notions of self-esteem. We are to repudiate or renounce all self-sufficiency. This is especially necessary for accomplishing anything of ultimate value. And if contentment is found in Christ and Christ alone, then the pursuit of something apart from his will and provision is a fool's errand.

Putting It Together

When we put this together we see that in ourselves, especially as fallen human beings, we are nothing, deserve nothing, and can do nothing.

When you read a sentence like that, do you feel a slight reflex of self-justification? Often there are small undiscovered islands of self-righteousness in our hearts. Laying things out in a plain and straightforward manner helps us to learn the lessons of self-denial. I confess that thinking about these concepts makes me feel small and insignificant. But isn't this the first step to denying self? We must survey ourselves and get a proper appraisal. Truth be told, we are even *worse* than nothing because we have rebelled against God. It is worse to be opposed to what is good than simply to lack what is good. What's more, God himself does not need us and is not the better off with us. He is utterly sufficient and eternally happy in himself. He displays his love to us in such a heart-melting, pride-smashing way that we are amazed by his grace. He speaks words of love when he tells us to deny ourselves and follow Jesus. Putting off the old self means putting on "the new self, created after the likeness of God in true righteousness and holiness" (Eph. 4:24). "Whoever loses his life for [Jesus's] sake will find it" (Matt. 10:39).

Doesn't this put things in perspective? Like visiting the optometrist and being asked whether a lens is "better or worse," revisiting the need for self-denial puts the question of contentment in sharper focus. Jesus is the source of all true and abiding contentment. He has that in himself. He stands before a world that is running on empty and says, "If anyone would come after me, let him deny himself." That is, if anyone would line up with me and be filled with me, he must first deny his self-centeredness and self-sufficiency.

Do you see how important this realization is? God wills that he be the source of your contentment. He has always willed this, ever since the garden of Eden. And now in Christ he draws near to us through the gospel and says, "You must deny yourself." It is one of the many ironies of the gospel: deny yourself and be found content in Christ; deny Christ and find yourself restlessly lost in yourself.

A Reception

We should not miss the fact that the call to deny self is also a call to follow Christ. God does not simply call us to repudiate ourselves. Instead, he calls us to repudiate ourselves and to receive him—and with him, our true identity. These are words of conviction and grace that pursue us amid our confusion. Like Adam and Eve clinging to their fig leaves, we cling to our selfishness. And God pursues us in grace and calls us to put aside the folly and look to him.

It is helpful to consider who God calls us to look upon when we deny ourselves. It is the Lord Jesus Christ. Let's not forget that Jesus spoke these words of instruction not from heaven but from right here on earth. The second person of the Trinity became a man. He was born of the Virgin Mary but remained fully God while also being wholly man. His incarnation is not only a repudiation of our best but also the arrival of God's best! He came "for us and our salvation," as the Nicene Creed says.

God became a man in Christ in order to live the life you and I could not and would not live. Paul is adamant to make this point in Romans 3:10–23. Summarizing, he says,

> None is righteous, no, not one;
> > no one understands;
> > no one seeks for God.
> All have turned aside; together they have become worthless;
> > no one does good,
> > not even one. (3:10–12)

But Jesus came to obey God's law for lawbreakers like you and me. He came to love the unlovely and the unloving. He came to save sinners. And he fully discharged his duty as the second Adam. Unlike the first Adam, Jesus fully kept and honored God's law (John 4:34; 8:29; 17:3–4). In his obedience, he earned the righteousness that we so desperately need.

Christ also went to the cross. Because we are so utterly helpless and hopeless, left unto ourselves, we need a Savior who can do what God requires. Our sin not only created a lack of righteousness but also earned a death penalty (Rom. 6:23). Therefore, if God was going to forgive anyone, his righteous judgment had to be satisfied. The wrath of God was rightly directed toward us. We earned it. But Christ, moved by love and in obedience to his Father, went to the cross for us. There upon the cross, Jesus endured hell on earth. He bore the unmitigated, undiluted, fully fermented cup of divine wrath. As the hymn writer Philip Bliss expressed it:

> Bearing shame and scoffing rude,
> in my place condemned he stood;

sealed my pardon with his blood.
Hallelujah! What a Savior![7]

Every one of our sins and every second of their eternal penalty were poured into this cup of eternal wrath. Charles Spurgeon explains:

> His love for his people was so strong, that he took the cup in both hands, and at one tremendous draught of love, he drank damnation dry for all his people. He drank it all, he endured all, he suffered all; so that now for ever there are no flames of hell for them, no racks of torment; they have no eternal woes; Christ hath suffered all they ought to have suffered, and they must, they shall go free.[8]

After bowing his head in death, he was placed in a tomb. But death could not contain him. On the third day, Christ victoriously and powerfully rose from the dead. He conquered sin, Satan, and death. The seed of the woman had triumphed over the seed of the Serpent. Christ had risen from the dead to give life to his people!

When we put this together, we see that on our own we are very needy. We lack righteousness, atonement, and the ability to defeat death. However, in Christ we get everything! As Sinclair Ferguson put it, "Everything we need and everything we lack is found in Christ."[9]

This call of Christ to deny ourselves is a call of faith. It is a call to appraise ourselves based on the scale and measure of God's Word, and then to apply the same measure to Christ. Such a comparison shows how much we are lacking and how completely Christ supplies our need. In the words of Octavius Winslow:

> His fullness meets my emptiness. His blood cleanses my guilt. His grace subdues my sin. His patience bears with my infirmi-

7. Philip P. Bliss, "Hallelujah! What a Savior!," 1875.
8. Charles H. Spurgeon, "Justification by Grace," sermon 126 in *The New Park Street Pulpit Sermons*, vol. 3 (London: Passmore & Alabaster, 1857), 155.
9. Sinclair Ferguson, "Our New Affection," *Tabletalk*, December, 2015, 22.

ties. His gentleness succours my weakness. His love quickens my obedience. His sympathy soothes my sorrows. His beauty charms my eye. He is just the Savior, just the Christ I need, and no words can describe His preciousness to my soul![10]

To see your need of Christ and his willingness to save you creates an explosion of happiness in the soul.

Heaven is so happy because those who are there have come to see, without any impediments or weights of sin, that God is their all in all. In heaven there is eternal delight without the things we so often chase after. We worry so much about money, clothes, food, housing, employment, relationships, and whatever will come tomorrow. There is no need to worry about anything in heaven because faith has become sight and promise has become fulfillment. But what about life in this world? Are we not enjoying the blessings of knowing God here and now? The first glance of faith upon Christ is a look that esteems his worth and repudiates self-worth. This also is the sight of those in heaven. The challenge we have in the meantime, as we chase contentment throughout our lives, is to deny ourselves by looking away from ourselves and unto Christ.

Practicing Ongoing Self-Denial

The posture of self-denial that is vital as we enter the kingdom is also vital to living as kingdom citizens. Here are some practical considerations.

Remember What Self-Indulgence Brings

Imagine yourself back in the garden. You are standing there with Adam, near enough to Eve to hear the Serpent's crafty temptation. Knowing what you know now about sin and its effects, what would you say? You would rush into the scene and shout, "No! Don't do it! It's a trap! Deny yourself!"

---

10. Octavius Winslow, *The Precious Things of God* (London: Nisbet, 1861), 19 (spelling and punctuation adapted).

This side of Genesis 3 we know that "the wages of sin is death" (Rom. 6:23). We know the costliness of redemption. We know that while sin promises fullness and pleasure, it leaves us hungry and hurting. We know that every single problem in the world today traces back to the first sin. Self-indulgence is the mother of hell, and it is the tireless longing of our flesh. Let's not forget that our flesh is the internal ally of the Devil, and it tempts us relentlessly (James 1:13–15). Beware of the endgame of self-indulgence and the insatiable desire of the flesh. When you do, you will want to deny it.

Remember What You Really Need

In the practice of self-denial I am encouraged by two things. First, we don't need very much. Jesus taught us to pray for daily bread. Paul said if we have food and shelter, we should be content. God feeds the birds, clothes the lilies, and cares for his children. But as Thomas Watson said, "The stomach is sooner filled than the eye."[11] In other words, our lusts are insatiable. Therefore, focus on what you need and be thankful for it. Second, God has not kept back from you anything you need. When we are self-indulgent, we often pursue things beyond what God has promised—or worse, contrary to what he has promised. How much would our lusts diminish if we restricted them to what God has promised!

Remember What Jesus Died to Bring

We should never forget that Jesus came to free us from our sin and its penalty. In his incarnation Christ denied himself so that we could be freed from sin, not fat from it. The Christian's new life in the Spirit is empowered to continually deny self and pursue God. The sixth chapter of Romans reminds us that we who were formerly slaves to sin have now been set free to be slaves of

---

11. Thomas Watson, *The Art of Divine Contentment: An Exposition of Philippians 4:11*, chap. 14, rule 14, accessed July 5, 2016, http://www.biblebb.com/files/TW/tw-contentment.htm.

righteousness (Rom. 6:18–19). Self-denial is central to the life in the Spirit.

Remember the Practice of Self-Denial

Watson helpfully says that we are to mortify our desires and moderate our delights.[12] *Mortify* simply means kill or put to death (Col. 3:5). When you put a desire to death, you are removing its appetite. A dead man is not a hungry man. To do this, we must do two things well, says Watson.

First, our desires need to be guided by reality. We need to have a biblically formed worldview. What is right? What is true? What is beautiful? When we are convinced of the matter biblically, then we will pursue it.

Second, we need to remember how short life is. Death is coming, whether we like it or not. Sooner than we may estimate, death will "crop these flowers which we delight in, and pull down the fabric of those bodies which we so garnish and beautify."[13] We need a proper perspective on the world.

We must also moderate our delights. Because we were made to love, we find ourselves loving people and things very much. But we should heed the caution, "Rachel set her heart too much upon her children, and when she had lost them, she lost herself too; such a vein of grief was opened as could not be staunched, 'she refused to be comforted.'"[14] If we are not careful, we can turn good things like close relationships into ultimate things. God's gifts can again replace God himself. And when he then takes them away, we become undone.

Reduce Your Desires to Fit Your Circumstances

Often our desires (even good desires) outrun our experience. This can lead to great disappointment. Consider a young woman who

12. Ibid., chap. 14, rule 5.
13. Ibid.
14. Ibid.

desperately wants to be married, but God, in his providence, has not yet brought her a husband. What if her happiness is bound up in having a husband? She absolutely cannot be content without him. Certainly God would have this child of his find her contentment in her Lord, even amid this admittedly good desire. In this situation she would need to subordinate her marital desire to the present situation of being single. Subordinating otherwise good desires is hard work, but it is a work of grace. God brings people to a place where they can say, "I want to be married, but God has not yet brought me a spouse. He is good and wise. I trust his timing and pray that he would be so kind as to answer my prayer."

This is the path of humility and trust. It is absolutely contrary to the way most people think. Most people say they'd be happy if they could just have more. But God often makes us content not by giving us more stuff or relationships but by giving us more humility and trust. We want to be promoted, but the path of contentment is to be brought lower.

— — —

As with so much of the Christian life, Jesus is the model and the motivation for our obedience. He denied himself so that we could have life in him. He was made nothing that we could be something. He was empty that we would be filled. Now he calls us to follow him in obedience, hearing again and again his command to deny ourselves and follow him.

Review Questions

1. What does it mean to deny yourself?

2. In terms of learning contentment, why is this essential?

3. How does a biblically informed worldview of what is right, true, and beautiful inform your self-denial?

4. How does actively working to subordinate your desires to your circumstances reflect humility and trust in God?

5. Make a list of things or circumstances that may tempt you into discontentment. How does Christ serve as your model and motivation for self-denial?

7

Be Still and Know

Recently I was teaching a conference on evangelism. After one of the sessions a dear couple in their seventies came up to talk about their burden for the lost in their family and community. Throughout our conversation, they talked about the Lord's goodness. At one point, with eyes full of tears, the woman said, "We have lost two of our sons." She paused to gather herself, then continued, "But the Lord has been so good to us through all of this." The couple went on to tell how the Lord had graciously sustained them through two unexpected and particularly heart-wrenching events. They were not yet through these trials or the pain of loss. But even though God's plans upended theirs, they continued to trust, love, and rest in him. They remained content in God.

Not only our difficulties but also our seasons of blessing must be viewed in light of who God is. I have a friend who is a business owner and over the last couple of years has seen his company grow substantially. When things were taking off, I asked him about how he was handling his success. His response surprised me. Instead of saying that everything was great, he confessed his personal pride, restlessness for more, and even coldness toward the Lord. Though it's tempting to think that abundant blessings will cure all of our problems, in my friend's case, the blessings served to reveal a problem of discontentment.

When considered biblically, both seasons of blessing and seasons of affliction provide opportunities to learn contentment in God. Isn't this what the apostle Paul shared with the Philippians in his letter to them? "Not that I am speaking of being in need, for I have learned in whatever situation I am to be content. I know how to be brought low, and I know how to abound. In any and every circumstance, I have learned the secret of facing plenty and hunger, abundance and need" (Phil. 4:11–12). Paul experienced both ends of the stick: abundance and affliction. Each circumstance drove him back to God, the source of his contentment.

But here is the question: What is it about God that made Paul content? What did he know that helped him interpret his circumstances and be able to say, "I have learned in whatever situation I am to be content"? One of the keys for Paul was a healthy understanding and application of God's providence.

Providence might be a new word for you, and if it is, I hope it quickly becomes a favorite. It's an important word we Christians need to know and delight in. Often we define the hard words of our faith and then quickly replace them. In doing so, we risk losing something of our history and even core elements of our faith. At one time, this word was so prevalent in people's minds that they named cities after it.[1]

What does *providence* mean? In short, it refers to God's work in which he upholds, governs, and sustains all things by his infinite power. The definition from the Heidelberg Catechism bears repeating:

> God's providence is his almighty and ever present power, whereby, as with his hand, he still upholds heaven and earth and all creatures, and so governs them so that: leaf and blade, rain and drought, fruitful and barren years, food and drink,

---

1. E.g., Providence, Rhode Island.

health and sickness, riches and poverty, indeed, all things, come to us not by chance but by his fatherly hand.[2]

The main thing to remember about God's providence is that he is not disconnected from or disinterested in what is happening in the world today. There is no such thing as chance, luck, or fate. Rather, God is upholding, governing, and ordering all things with his very hand.[3] Nothing escapes God's sovereign control. Whatever he pleases he does (Ps. 135:6), and whatever he does he pleases. He works all things according to the counsel of his own will (Eph. 1:11). The execution of this will is God's providence.

Providence and Contentment

Let's think about the doctrine of providence in reference to our understanding of contentment. You may recall that contentment is the inward, gracious, quiet spirit that joyfully rests in God's providence. This plays out in Scripture in several ways. In the letter to the Hebrews we read, "Keep your life free from love of money, and be content with what you have, for he has said, 'I will never leave you nor forsake you'" (Heb. 13:5). How does this text relate to God's providence? When the Bible says be content with what you have, it basically is saying, "Be content with what God has given you." In other words, rest in God's providence. This becomes pivotal to our pursuit of contentment.

If we are going to recover the experience of Christian contentment, we must recover the doctrine of God's providence. According to the writer of Hebrews, the two are inextricably linked. A heart that is content is a heart that rests in God's providence. To put it another way, the inward work of grace in believers gives them eyes to see and interpret what is happening in the world

---

2. Heidelberg Catechism, Lord's Day 10.
3. The London Baptist Confession of Faith 5.2 is helpful along these lines: "Although in relation to the foreknowledge and decree of God, Who is the First Cause, all things come to pass immutably and infallibly; so that nothing happens to anyone by chance, or outside His providence, yet by His providence He orders events to occur according to the nature of second causes, either necessarily, freely, or contingently."

around them. Because the heart has been tuned by grace, is being filled with divine love, and is learning contentment, it rests in God's providence.

Since this doctrine is often underemphasized, it would be helpful to think through some aspects of providence with an eye toward our contentment in God.[4]

Nothing Escapes Providence

If we are going to embrace and esteem God's providence, we must understand the extent of it. Does God's providence only have to do with certain big things, or does it include everything? The answer is crucial for our understanding of contentment.

The Bible teaches us not only that God rules the entire world and upholds the universe but also that he is involved with the seemingly minute details of life. What an astounding reality! The same God who hung the stars in the sky also knows the number of hairs on your head and keeps his eye on the sparrow (Luke 12:6–7). God's providence is not merely a general oversight of the world but applies to everything and everyone. It reaches into every home, to every member of the family, and to every meal on the table. It extends to everything that happens to us and our neighbors. Jesus communicates the extent of God's providence by pointing to sparrows and the hairs on our head. These things are inconsequential to us but not to God.

Providence also extends to things we might not label as good. Everything that comes to pass comes from God's fatherly hand. Depending on your circumstances, this may be a difficult pill to swallow; but it is nevertheless true and therefore important for our understanding of who God is and how he works. I will build out implications of this shortly, but for now, it is crucial for our pursuit of contentment to understand that nothing escapes God's providence.

---

4. Some of what follows expands upon and updates material found in Jeremiah Burroughs, *The Rare Jewel of Christian Contentment* (Edinburgh: Banner of Truth, 1979).

Nothing Hinders Providence

One of the symptoms of discontent is complaining against circumstances. When the nation of Israel was making the trek from Egypt to the Promised Land, the people were unhappy with the food choices. They began grumbling and complaining (Ex. 16:1ff.). But to whom were they grumbling? Moses admonished them, "Your grumbling is not against us but against the LORD" (Ex. 16:8). In the New Testament, Jesus reminded his disciples that no amount of worrying can bring change (Matt. 6:27).

Suppose circumstances have fallen out in a way that you did not anticipate. You're unhappy, impatient, and restless. You want things to be different. Do you really believe that providence should change its course to suit you? Let's remember that the hand you've been dealt has come from God's own wise and good hand. Furthermore, it comes from his powerful hand. We have neither the right nor the power to grumble against God. We may shake our heads at the Israelites' petulance about their rations in the wilderness, but what about us when we receive an unfavorable medical diagnosis or find ourselves betrayed by a friend? Can we make one hair on our head black or white with all our frustration and worry? Jeremiah Burroughs draws this comparison:

> When you are in a ship at sea which has all its sails spread with a full gale of wind, and is swiftly sailing, can you make it stand still by running up and down in the ship? No more can you make the providence of God alter and change its course with your vexing and fretting; it will go on with power, do what you can.[5]

Providence Comes from a Good God

The first two realities, if taken alone, might tend to discourage rather than encourage you. God's providence extends to everything and you cannot thwart it. But what kind of God stands

5. Ibid., 112–13.

behind this providence? Is he good or malicious? How are we to understand our circumstances in light of who God is? These are key questions that must be answered before we can rest in the providence of God. In fact, doubting God's goodness is often a veiled symptom of discontentment. Like the wandering Israelites in the wilderness, we don't connect the dots and see that grumbling about our circumstances is grumbling about God's character.

The Bible teaches us that in addition to being all-powerful, God is both good and wise. The psalmist prayed, "You are good and do good" (Ps. 119:68). In fact, God's goodness is meant to evoke our praise (Ps. 107:1). We are to look at who God is and then evaluate what he does. Therefore, whatever we think about our circumstances, we must remember that no matter what, God is good and he has—for some reason, often unknown to us—allowed these things to come to pass. Resting in God's providence is resting in a good God.

Providence Comes from a Wise God

We can become restless and even question God's wisdom when events just don't seem to add up or another path looks more favorable. This is often the biggest struggle for me. So I have to remember at such times that this God who stands behind all his works of providence is no less powerful, good, and wise. And this means that if another option were truly better, he would have ensured that it happened.

This type of thinking may raise a lot of questions. For example, take any news story that provokes a response like "Oh no, that's horrible!" Whether it's terrorist actions like the September 11 attacks or a surprising diagnosis of cancer to a young parent, we can agree that these things are heartbreaking. How can they be part of God's plan?

This is where we must remember that we are living in a post–Genesis 3 world. This world is cursed because of sin. It is a broken world—a world with death, disease, and disaster. Many of the things that happen in this world directly contradict what the Bible reveals as God's will for morality and life. Does this mean that these things are a surprise to God? Of course not. Does it mean that God is the author of evil? No, definitely not. Then how can God be said to be sovereign over everything and yet not be responsible for the evil that people commit or the disaster that people endure? The simple answer is that these things are above our mental pay grade. They are beyond our understanding—but not beyond God's. "The secret things belong to the LORD our God, but the things that are revealed belong to us and to our children" (Deut. 29:29).

The Bible indicates that God stands behind all good in such a way that he is the primary cause of it, and therefore he is to receive glory for and through it (cf. James 1:17). However, he stands behind evil, not in a primary sense but in a secondary sense. People do what they want to do, and God, in his wisdom and power, is able to work these things together for his glory and our good. The most obvious example of this is the cross of Jesus Christ. God predestined it to occur, but those who committed the crime were responsible for the action (Acts 2:22–23). God is sovereign and men are responsible. God works from within a broken system to glorify himself and do good to people.

When we settle in our minds the issue that God is good and wise, we can truly rest in his providence. This means we can be content whether things go our way or God seems to have gone against what we have planned. We calm our hearts and rest in him. We sit still, knowing that he is the all-powerful, good, and wise God.

Providence Is Varied but Purposeful

When we think about the scope of God's providence, we can scarcely begin to grasp it. In October 2012 the world's population reached 7 billion people. Some population experts have estimated the total number of people who have lived thus far to be 107 billion.[6] This means that not only is God the Creator of all of these people but he was working all the details together and intimately familiar with every single person on every single day. This is too difficult to fathom.

With all of this time, all these people, and all these events, there seem to be an infinite number of works of God's ordinary providence. Yet, all of them work together in an orderly way. God orchestrates billions and billions of interdependent events as if they are one combined event. Burroughs puts it this way:

> There are an infinite number of wheels, as I may say, in the works of providence; put together all the works that ever God did from all eternity or ever will do, and they all make up but one work, and they have been as several wheels that have had their orderly motion to attain the end that God from all eternity has appointed.[7]

We tend to look at things in chunks. We might consider our personal life, or our family and friends, or perhaps our place in the general arc of history. However, these are simply chapters in the one grand book of God's providence that extends from the beginning of creation (Genesis 1) until the current day. In other words, we may be tempted to look at God's providence as fragmented rather than consolidated. But God's providence is a unified divine act whereby he orders, upholds, and governs all things. Something that God does today in your life might surprise you, but you may begin to see its impact twenty-five years later. This is the way his providence works.

This holistic view also becomes a suitable vantage point for evaluating our discontent over the way God has seen fit to order our particular circumstances. In addition to whatever prompts our discontent, God is also doing millions of other things. To remove

6. Wesley Stephenson, "Do the Dead Outnumber the Living?," *BBC News*, February 4, 2012, http://www.bbc.com/news/magazine-16870579.

7. Burroughs, *The Rare Jewel of Christian Contentment*, 113.

our discontent and get the one thing we want, we might have to void God's plans for a thousand other things contingent on this one thing. We simply do not have the ability to understand the depth of God's providence. "Who has known the mind of the Lord . . . ?" (Rom. 11:34).

> For my thoughts are not your thoughts,
>   neither are your ways my ways, declares the LORD.
> For as the heavens are higher than the earth,
>   so are my ways higher than your ways
>   and my thoughts than your thoughts. (Isa. 55:8–9)

We are directed back to who God is and what he does. Instead of giving us what we might consider a sufficient explanation, Scripture gives us an all-sufficient person. As believers we are to rest in him.

In addition to being varied but unified, providence is also purposeful. As opposed to the randomness that characterizes luck or chance, providence is God's work with a particular goal in mind. We know that God does everything for the purpose of his glory (Isa. 42:8; 48:11; Eph. 1:5–6, 11–12). We can be assured that whatever happens, God is going to use it for his glory.

The pursuit of God's own glory is not distinct from the good he does for those who follow Christ. In other words, God's glory and our good are not mutually exclusive. The Bible teaches that God works all things together for the good of those who love him (Rom. 8:28). This is a tremendous promise to hold onto! Surely you can see how this aids us in our pursuit of contentment.

Recently a new family joined our church. Within a short time, the wife was diagnosed with breast cancer. With eyes full of tears, her husband told me of the diagnosis. Having gone through many different medical trials himself, he admitted that he did not know God's immediate purpose in this but said that he trusted him and knew that he would work it together for their good. In fact, when this man asked me to pray, he said, "Don't just pray for healing.

Pray for our hearts. Pray that our attitudes and actions would glorify God." In so many words he said, "What good would healing be if we dishonored Christ?"

The waves of life in a post–Genesis 3 world are unpredictable and frightening. However, we know that the God who calms the seas works through the storms for our good and his glory. This is our confidence amid the storm. We rest in the providence of God because God is sovereign, good, wise, and purposeful.

Become Familiar with How God Works

We have considered providence in general terms, but it is also helpful to consider more particularly how God often works out his providence in his people's lives. This helps to inform and perhaps even restrain our expectations. I remember, as a brand new pastor during a particularly trying period of time, asking a couple of older pastors, "Is it always like this?" They smiled reassuringly and said yes. I had a perception of pastoral ministry that while things were not going to be perfect or easy, they certainly weren't going to be perennially difficult! Was I wrong! Can you imagine how these false expectations could fuel discontent? Having proper expectations for what the Christian life is typically like aids us in our pursuit of contentment. When this is coupled with a biblical understanding of who God is and why ultimately he does what he does, then we find ourselves learning contentment.

Here I will highlight a few traits that seem to characterize God's ways with his people.

Expect a Stiff Headwind

Jesus reminds us disciples that life is going to be hard (John 16:33). But this difficulty is not simply because the world is cursed; it is also because God is doing something. The trials and afflictions we face are not surprises to God but purposeful tools to strengthen our faith and make us content in him.

A few years ago I used a bicycle as my primary transportation.

This meant that I was regularly checking the forecast for rain, snow, and—most importantly—wind. If I had a tailwind, I could knock several minutes off my commute, but if I had a headwind, then I was going to have work harder. One day amid my griping about the trend of having a stiff headwind on both the way in and the way home from work, a friend quipped, "How do you think you get stronger?" His point was clear: the wind may have been a temporary inconvenience, but in light of some personal goals, it was actually serving me quite well. I would do better to embrace it and stop complaining.

God often brings a stiff headwind to us in our Christian lives. In fact, as I sit here I am presently feeling the pinch of about seven trials. As I consider some close friends, I can tally up another twenty-five or so. When I consider our church family, we are now talking about more than I can keep track of. Why do you suppose God does this? Is there a purpose? Like everything else in his workings with us, each trial is lovingly brought for a purpose. "Count it all joy, my brothers, when you meet trials of various kinds, for you know that the testing of your faith produces steadfastness. And let steadfastness have its full effect, that you may be perfect and complete, lacking in nothing" (James 1:2–4).

Here we see that the trials are purposeful. God uses each difficulty to grow, shape, and strengthen us. We might be tempted to complain about the difficulty we are facing. However, we learn in the Scripture that God lovingly and purposefully brings trials to build our faith. John Newton's wonderful hymn "I Asked the Lord" communicates this truth:

> I asked the Lord that I might grow
> In faith, and love, and every grace;
> Might more of His salvation know,
> And seek, more earnestly, His face.
>
> 'Twas He who taught me thus to pray,
> And He, I trust, has answered prayer!

But it has been in such a way,
As almost drove me to despair.

I hoped that in some favored hour,
At once He'd answer my request;
And by His love's constraining pow'r,
Subdue my sins, and give me rest.

Instead of this, He made me feel
The hidden evils of my heart;
And let the angry pow'rs of hell
Assault my soul in every part.

Yea more, with His own hand He seemed
Intent to aggravate my woe;
Crossed all the fair designs I schemed,
Blasted my gourds, and laid me low.

Lord, why is this, I trembling cried,
Wilt thou pursue thy worm to death?
"'Tis in this way," the Lord replied,
"I answer prayer for grace and faith.

"These inward trials I employ,
From self, and pride, to set thee free;
And break thy schemes of earthly joy,
That thou may'st find thy all in Me."

Mercy Runs Downhill

Think about some of the great demonstrations of God's mercy in the Bible. When God appointed Joseph to leadership in Egypt, he had previously been abandoned in a pit and then wrongly imprisoned. Before being promoted by the king, Daniel found himself in the lion's den. David was promised the kingdom but was hunted like an animal in the wilderness. Let us not forget that our heritage as believers includes difficulty but that in such difficulty, God often sends his mercy flowing downhill to meet us at our lowest point.

We often see the godly afflicted, only to be flooded by the surprising river of God's mercy.

In his hymn "God Moves in a Mysterious Way," William Cowper showed the mystery of providence and the surprising bestowal of mercy God's his children:

> God moves in a mysterious way
> His wonders to perform;
> He plants His footsteps in the sea
> And rides upon the storm.
>
> Deep in unfathomable mines
> Of never failing skill
> He treasures up His bright designs
> And works His sov'reign will.
>
> Ye fearful saints, fresh courage take;
> The clouds ye so much dread
> Are big with mercy and shall break
> In blessings on your head.
>
> Judge not the Lord by feeble sense,
> But trust Him for His grace;
> Behind a frowning providence
> He hides a smiling face.
>
> His purposes will ripen fast,
> Unfolding every hour;
> The bud may have a bitter taste,
> But sweet will be the flow'r.

He Never Leaves Us

In Hebrews 13:5, quoted earlier, we are given a wonderful promise of God's abiding presence with us: "Keep your life free from love of money, and be content with what you have, for he has said, 'I will never leave you nor forsake you.'" Here is a promise amid the difficulties of life.

Think about how this promise comes to be yours. The reason you can truly be content in God is that you have this precious promise: he will not leave you. This reality did not come cheaply. Jesus Christ, our Savior and God's Son, was forsaken upon the cross. He was abandoned in judgment so that you would never be. He cried out, "My God, my God, why have you forsaken me?" (Matt. 27:46) so that you could say, "My God, my God, you have never forsaken me!" Contentment rooted in God's presence is costly and therefore gloriously precious, as expressed in this prayerful hymn:

> Abide with me; fast falls the eventide;
> The darkness deepens; Lord with me abide.
> When other helpers fail and comforts flee,
> Help of the helpless, O abide with me.
>
> Hold Thou Thy cross before my closing eyes;
> Shine through the gloom and point me to the skies.
> Heaven's morning breaks, and earth's vain shadows flee;
> In life, in death, O Lord, abide with me.[8]

Are You Discontent?

We could think in terms of three main categories of discontentment with God's providence in our personal histories. Not surprisingly they involve things that are happening, have happened, and will happen. Here are some questions to ask yourself.

Am I grumbling about the present? If we are grumbling about something we're going through right now, we are arguing with God. We are saying that we shouldn't have to endure this. Our present experiences are like a magnet drawing out either our discontentment or our contentment. If we are grumbling, we can be sure we are not content. We are essentially saying that God is getting it wrong. Such discontentment questions God's wisdom, goodness, and power.

---

8. Henry F. Lyte, "Abide with Me," 1847.

Am I bitter about the past? Everyone has faced hard days. Some people's pasts are harder than others, but all have felt the sting of sin and pain in our fallen world. Many people live under the cloud of their past hardships and become increasingly bitter. Over time they revisit and analyze the situations from the perspective of a victim, only to feed their bitterness. We cannot be content in the present when we are nursing bitterness about the past. We are basically saying that God failed us. This discontentment too questions God's wisdom, goodness, and power.

Am I worrying about the future? What is going to happen tomorrow? How do I know it's really going to be okay? Where will I work? Whom will I marry? We can ask hundreds of questions about the future, but the bottom line is that we don't know. And we can't know. Sadly, many people sit in bondage to worry about the future and lose the joy of contentment in the present. Jesus saw this as the trait of the unbeliever (Matt. 6:25–34) rather than the believer, who knows and trusts God. If we are worrying, we are as much as saying that God won't get it right. This is yet another form of discontentment that questions God's wisdom, goodness, and power.

Rest in the God of Providence and the Providence of God

How do we counsel others and ourselves in such states? We must remember the providence of God and the God of providence. That means remembering that God is upholding and governing all things. He is purposely involved in the details. So whatever happened, is happening, or will happen comes with divine sanction. What's more, Christians in particular should be encouraged to know that God's providence means he is working all things together for his glory and our good (Rom. 8:28). When I am discontent about the past, the present, or the future, I am bucking against God's rule, questioning his wisdom, and doubting his love. If we are discontent, we must remember the comforting doctrine of God's providence.

We must also remember the *God* of providence. God is a good God who is as wise as he is in control. All too often we interpret God's character in light of our circumstances. When things are going well, we think that God is good and that he loves us. However, when things don't go our way, we often feel like God is unfair and doesn't want what is best for us. Restlessness ferments in our hearts, and before we know it, we are questioning his goodness.

Have you felt this temptation? Instead of interpreting God's character in light of our circumstances, we must do the opposite and interpret our circumstances in light of God's character. We must take the thread of our situation and run it through the needle of God's character. This will assure us that even though our situation is difficult and not what we would have chosen, God is nevertheless in full control, absolutely good, and powerfully directing this experience for his glory and our good. There are no wasted hardships with God—everything has a purpose.

Finally, when considering God's providence, we must remember the chief display of providence, the cross of Christ. The ultimate medicine for our souls is the cross. It is the Visine that removes the irritation from the eyes of our souls and focuses our sight clearly upon the truth. The cross dramatizes what we deserve. We do not deserve mercy, but we get it. God intervened in our perennial party of selfishness and nailed our sin to the cross (Col. 2:14). We can never clamor about what we deserve when we are standing in the shadow of the cross. The cross reminds us that Jesus got what we deserve and we get what Jesus deserved. It's hard to complain when you remember that you deserve hell.

But the cross also assures us that God can be trusted. Isn't this the central issue for us? Can you trust God? Well, stand again in the shadow of the cross and let the apostle interpret it for you and apply it to our life's experiences: "He who did not spare his own Son but gave him up for us all, how will he not also with him graciously give us all things?" (Rom. 8:32).

If you can trust God to take care of the biggest issues—sin and death—then you can trust him to take care of you in the secondary matters—everything else.

– – –

If we are to learn contentment, we have to be able to spot discontentment. If we are grumbling, bitter, or worrying, then we can be sure we are discontent. We need to run back to the Scriptures to find our rest in the providence of God and the God of providence.

Review Questions

1. What is providence?

2. What is the link between your contentment and divine providence?

3. What do you know about God's character (and therefore his providence) that can cause you to be content in any circumstance?

4. What do bitterness, grumbling, and anxiety reveal about your relationship with God and your understanding of providence?

5. How does the cross inform and shape your understanding of God's providence?

8

Be a Faithful Bride

What role does your church have in your pursuit of contentment? Your church has a primary role. Does this surprise you? Think about where the battle lines are drawn in your pursuit. Contentment is about whether or not you will rest and rejoice in the sufficiency of the Trinity or will fall for the deceptive marketing of this fallen world. Will you fasten your heart supremely upon created things (people, stuff, etc.), or will you be content in God? God uses the church to help make the latter a reality. In this chapter I want to show why this is true and how it happens. I will also aim to show you how the Enemy and our flesh work to undermine our pursuit of contentment.

Let's think together about church and, in particular, the congregation where you are a member.[1] If it is like most churches today, it is not very large (probably fewer than two hundred people). You may be tempted to think that your church, with its modest size, is rather insignificant. When I talk to people about their churches, I almost sense a little embarrassment about the

---

1. Because I am writing to Christians, or at least showing curious readers how Christians learn contentment, I am assuming that readers are members of gospel-preaching churches. There is no biblical concept of being a member of the universal church without being a member of a local church.

size and perceived scope of their church. Apologetic words like *small* and *ordinary* come up. These words are not derogatory at all—and perhaps even accurate—but the sentiment behind them is concerning, especially in light of how the church serves to help you learn contentment.

When you read that word *ordinary*, what do you think of? Common synonyms include *unimpressive*, *typical*, *normal*, and *common*: as in "My day was typical." "The movie was unimpressive." "The book was average." When you think about the church in general and your congregation in particular, you might be a bit embarrassed by its ordinariness. But what if you don't have thousands of members, a massive building, or the reputation for being the "cool church"? What if you are just a church? What if you are an ordinary ministry? Is this okay?

Here is the bottom-line reality: the church is the most important organization on the planet. Its importance and inherent value are dependent not upon size but upon substance. The church equips its members to answer the highest calling on the planet—to glorify God, by helping people to know and follow Jesus (Matt. 28:19–21). There is nothing more noble or important than this. This does not impugn the importance of other organizations that likewise do very good things, but it does relativize them. Nothing takes the place of prominence like the church. The church is the bride of Christ.

Furthermore, the church has the greatest collective impact. While many organizations may boast of real help for people in this world (and I praise God for them), only the church can truly say that it brings help in this world and the next. The church is involved in rescuing sinners from an eternity in hell. Think about this: we rejoice when a group is able to help people get over addictions and enjoy a meaningful life. But, as good as this is, freedom from addiction, by itself, has an impact for only a few decades. How much more does the church shine in her mission to seek and save the lost from eternal suffering? And the church too has a tremendous impact on this present life. As Christians gather and work together to hear and apply God's Word, they encourage each other to be content in God. They grow together in Christ and thus grow in contentment.

Whom God Uses—"Not Many Wise"

God's magnificence work in and through the church seems counterintuitive considering whom God uses and how he does it.

At the risk of understatement, the Corinthian church had issues. But it had issues because it was made up of sinners. One problem was their penchant for exalting people and then identifying with them (to give them a sense of status). Even in the church, there arose various personality cults (1 Cor. 3:1–6). One person said, "I am of Apollos." Another said, "I am of Paul." Someone else boasted, "I am of Cephas."

Can you see what a problem this would be? After all, the church is supposed to be united under a common Savior, serving a common mission, and saluting the same gospel flag. Instead the Corinthians were acting like fanboys of their favorite pop icons. This immaturity brought about the fleshly fruit of jealousy, arguments, and bitterness (1 Cor. 3:3). Many in the church were producing this bad fruit. And as is always the case, those governed by the flesh were drawn to this like single-minded fruit flies.

The church exists to glorify God by helping people to know and follow Jesus. We do this by means of the ministry of the Word of God. The result of this, by God's grace, is that people grow and look more and more like Christ. We become conformed to his image (Eph. 4:11–15). But what are we being "deconformed" from (if I can use that term) as we are being conformed to Christ? It is self. Sadly, in Corinth the very thing that the church should endeavor to cultivate was being seditiously undermined by a dangerous knockoff. Instead of cultivating contentment in their Creator through the gospel, they were pursuing contentment in creation through personality cults.

What was their chief issue? They had bad memories. They suffered from a gospel amnesia that brought about Christian apathy. They had forgotten who Christ was and what he had done (1 Cor. 1:26–31). But they had also forgotten who they were. The apostle lovingly refreshes their memories:

> For consider your calling, brothers: not many of you were wise according to worldly standards, not many were powerful, not many were of noble birth. But God chose what is foolish in the world to shame the wise; God chose what is weak in the world to shame the strong; God chose what is low and despised in the world, even things that are not, to bring to nothing things that are, so that no human being might boast in the presence of God. And because of him you are in Christ Jesus, who became to us wisdom from God, righteousness and sanctification and redemption, so that, as it is written, "Let the one who boasts, boast in the Lord." (1 Cor. 1:26–31)

Did you catch what Paul does here? He accents the greatness of Christ by reminding the Corinthians that they really aren't very impressive. Christ's awesomeness, when rightly perceived, has an uncanny ability to show us that we are not very awesome. At the same time, Paul does not diminish the church. The church, after all, is the means by which the gospel goes forth. To put it another way, the beauty of the church is seen in the preciousness of the gospel she preaches and the weakness of those who preach it. It is as if Paul is saying, "You didn't get into this by being great and impressive. You got in because God is rich in mercy to those who are neither great nor impressive."

How God Does It

We've all encountered advertisements for a fast path to better health or a more fit body. The secrets, previously unknown to mankind for thousands of years, have now been discovered. All we have to do is click the ad and try the new program to have all our health and fitness dreams come true. Over the years I have been committed to exercise and healthy living. I've read and talked to a lot of experts. What I've found is surprisingly simple: you need to work at it. Regular exercise and a healthy diet are what the experts tell us we need. It's what they have always told us. I remember my grandfather saying, "There is no substitute for hard work and discipline." It's still true. And the same is true in the church.

In Ephesians 4 we read of God's blueprint for his church. The goal, simply stated, is maturity: "mature manhood, to the measure of the fullness of Christ" (4:13). The means by which this happens is the proper functioning of the body of Christ (4:16). But how does the body function properly? It does so as its members speak the truth to one another, having been properly equipped by those gifted in teaching the Word of God (4:11–15). In short, God wants his people to become mature in the Word, in the context of the local church, by means of the sound teaching and application of his Word.

At this point you might be thinking, *Okay, I agree with you about the importance of a faithful local church. But what does this specifically have to do with my contentment?* This is a vastly important question. Think back to the garden of Eden. Adam was given a plot of land and told to be a steward over it (Gen. 2:15). Genesis indicates that the garden was to spread. Adam and Eve were to be fruitful and multiply and fill the earth (Gen. 1:28). If they had persisted in obedience and spread out to corners of the earth, the earth would have been filled with the glory of the Lord. This was God's design in creation. Adam, God's priest-king, was to promote and defend the holiness of God by spreading his glory to the ends of the earth. Did he do this? No. In Genesis 3 we read that Adam and Eve sinned. They failed to treasure God and trust his word. Disobeying, they died.

Jesus is often referred to as the second or last Adam (1 Cor. 15:45–48). He came to undo and restore all that the first Adam broke. I believe that Paul was picking up on this continuity with the first Adam when he showed what Jesus would do through the church. Look at what Paul says in Ephesians 4:10: "He who descended is the one who also ascended far above all the heavens, that he might fill all things." Commentator Peter O'Brien observes:

> Christ fills the universe, not in some semi-physical sense, but by his mighty rule over all things (see on [Eph.] 1:22–23), a notion that is parallelled in the Old Testament where filling the universe, in this sense of exercising sovereign rule, is predicated of God: "'Do I not fill heaven and earth?' says the Lord" (Jer. 23:24). Here the idea is transferred to Christ: he fills the universe through the exercise of his lordship over everything. This entails his functioning as the powerful ruler over the principalities ([Eph.] 1:21), and giving grace and strength to his people (4:13, 15–16), through whom he fulfils his purposes.[2]

In other words, Jesus is the King over the entire universe. As the last Adam he has stretched out his sovereign rule so that nothing is outside his jurisdiction. He has won. The church is in the business of taking the ground that the King has won. He has conquered, and his churches, as his ambassadors, come speaking of his victory, bidding others to submit to his rule. The kingdom of Christ is advancing to the edge of the earth through the gospel. And once people come to Christ, they come and join others in the church, where they grow together under the good and sovereign rule of Jesus the King.

What does contentment have to do with the local church? Everything. True contentment comes through a true knowledge of Christ. The church is the means by which the gospel goes out and the context by which the gospel is applied. As the Scriptures are taught and applied, we grow together in Christlikeness. This is another way of saying we grow in contentment. Jesus was the

2. Peter Thomas O'Brien, *The Letter to the Ephesians*, The Pillar New Testament Commentary (Grand Rapids, MI: Eerdmans, 1999), 296–97.

most content man who ever lived. He treasured God and trusted his promises. So those who share in Christ come to be conformed to his likeness. We come to be strengthened by him as we increasingly reflect him (Phil. 4:13).

How does God shape us and makes us content in him? God has a very specific goal, and he has provided clear teaching on what contentment looks like.

Assure and Deter

In a recent men's Bible study at our church, I was teaching on the importance of the local church in the life of the Christian. One lesson point had to do with how we, individually and collectively, have a responsibility for one another's sanctification. We have the privilege of encouraging each other with God's promises while also warning of the consequences of disobeying God's Word.

This study was attended by a number of guys in the military, and one of them offered a military illustration. He talked about how essential it is for the military to assure and deter. Our weapon systems, intelligence, and even deployment serve to assure our allies of our commitment to them while also deterring our enemies from attacking us. His point, by way of illustration, was that the church exists to assure the Christian of God's goodness and faithfulness while also deterring sin and apostasy by likewise reminding us of God's holiness and faithfulness. In other words, the church family, when functioning properly, assures its members of the truth of God's Word while also deterring them from rebellion against it. God has given us a number of ways in which we can do this as a local church. We can break them into two categories: formal large gatherings and informal smaller group meetings.

Regular Assembly of Christians

The book of Hebrews is a sobering letter. The writer is very concerned that his readers might not continue in the faith. He sees definite parallels with Israel's wandering in the wilderness. In the third chapter the writer recounts the painful history of those who heard the word of God but did not respond to it with faith. The message is clear: don't be like those who died in the wilderness; they heard but did not believe. Instead, hear the word of God and see the sufficiency and supremacy of Christ (Heb. 3:7–19). Throughout the rest of the book the writer employs a number of ways to assure believers (the promises of God and preciousness of Christ) and to deter apostasy, or turning away from Jesus. What is so instructive for us is how the writer assigns responsibility for this. It is not an individual spiritual assignment but a project for the congregation.

In chapter 10 we read of the importance of prioritizing the gathering of the local church: "And let us consider how to stir up one another to love and good works, not neglecting to meet together, as is the habit of some, but encouraging one another, and all the more as you see the Day drawing near" (Heb. 10:24–25). Notice the twofold emphasis: be sure to meet together and encourage one another when you meet. Most would see this as a reference to the gathering of God's people on the Lord's Day each week (though it is not limited to this).

We might again be struck with how unimpressively ordinary this is. Each Sunday, week after week, you go to that familiar place with others who are members in your local church. You talk together, catch up on what the Lord is teaching you, and express how you trust him. You sit together in a room to hear and respond to the Bible. Someone reads Scripture, and there are prayers, songs, preaching, the Lord's Table, and sometimes baptisms. Rarely do you come away from such a meeting saying, "Wow! That was amazing! I never saw that coming! Oh, man." In other words, the Sunday morning gathering of believers is, in one sense, rather ordinary.

One person compared it to brushing his teeth. I've never run out of the bathroom in the morning to find my wife and say:

"You'll never believe what just happened. I brushed my teeth! I started on the back left and then worked my way to the front. I got the most surprisingly refreshing lather going in there. And, oh, man, let me tell you about the rinse; it was a full twenty-five-second swish. When have you ever had a twenty-five-second swish?" This would obviously be silly; nobody does this. But, here's the point: the fact that tooth brushing is a normal activity does not make it less important. It is an important part of our daily hygiene. It prevents gum disease, cavities, and of course, bad breath!

Faithful attendance in your local church might not seem like much on the face of it. In fact, it might seem like bringing a plastic fork to a gun battle when we think about what is at stake. After all, we are talking about matters of eternal significance. But this is precisely the wonder of it. God loves to use the simple, weak, even ordinary things in order to showcase his beauty, glory, and power. With so much on the line, the writer of Hebrews points to the sufficiency and supremacy of Christ. He bids his readers to not neglect so great a salvation (2:1–4) and to unite hearing with faith. And the context of doing this is your seemingly unremarkable local church.

When my friend Larry showed up on a Sunday morning a couple of years ago, he seemed like someone whose wife dragged him to church. He didn't look comfortable, and I often saw him keeping to himself. He kept coming back, though. Week after week he would sit there and be served by the ministry of the Word. Over time I noticed a change. When I preached, he was no longer looking at his phone or the ceiling, he was looking at me. He started to engage with me and others about the sermon. I saw him talking to people, opening up his home, and attending Bible studies. When I look back at the last couple of years, I don't know of any one guy who took Larry under his wing. He is a busy guy and has a demanding schedule. It seems clear to me that he was growing through the ministry of the Word of God on Sunday mornings. He grew right before my eyes. I can think of dozens of "Larrys" out there. God is faithful to use the weekly assembly of the church to grow his people like this.

God meets us in the weekly gathering of the church. He speaks to us through the Scriptures. He encourages us in singing. He reminds us of our seat at his banquet table through the Lord's Supper. In the gathering he assures us of his promises and deters us from sin.

Informal Smaller Gatherings

In addition to the gathering of the whole church together, the New Testament talks about our lives together on a smaller scale. The "one anothers" can be many or few. Christians are to consider how to help one another to grow in their trusting and treasuring of Jesus—in other words, to grow in their contentment of God above all things.

One way we can do this is by meeting together with another believer to read the Bible and pray. An excellent resource for this is David Helm's book *One-to-One Bible Reading*.[3] Helm helps equip and encourage readers to prioritize reading the Bible and praying together. Imagine what would happen in your church if people met each week to read and apply the Scriptures together in between your weekly gatherings.

In the church where I serve, we have encouraged this type of discipleship culture. When we see the biblical precedent and the biblical priority for discipleship, people become creative in arranging their schedules around loving and serving each other. I think of my own wife, who homeschools six children and serves heartily as a pastor's wife. She doesn't have a lot of time in the margin. After praying and carefully evaluating her schedule, she found that on one or two days per week during our kids' naptime she could meet with someone to read the Bible and pray. In the last two years I

---

3. David R. Helm, *One-to-One Bible Reading: A Simple Guide for Every Christian* (Kingsford, Australia: Matthias Media, 2011).

think she has missed only a handful of days meeting with women. Looking back, there is clear, evident fruit.

I think too of a brother in our church who faithfully invites people into his home. Often this hospitality leads to future meetings together for prayer and Bible reading. In the last couple of years I have watched several men grow while meeting with him. These are just a couple of the examples I have seen in my context. I am sure you have many stories in your church as well.

When we feel the weight of our accountability together and how costly sin is, love compels us into action. We have to prioritize the loving service of encouraging one another to rest in God's promises, rejoice in his goodness, and remain faithful to him. As the writer of Hebrews urged us, "Exhort one another every day, as long as it is called 'today,' that none of you may be hardened by the deceitfulness of sin" (Heb. 3:13).

Identifying Our Impediments to Faithfulness

An unfortunate reality hovers over this discussion: we often *don't* prioritize the local church. Christ's plan for his church is clear. Our instructions are not difficult. However, we avoid the church for the very reasons we need the church. That is the tendency of the fallen heart. What are some of those reasons?

Isolationism

In the same passage that talks about not neglecting the assembly, we read of how we are to intentionally love one another: "And let us consider how to stir up one another to love and good works" (Heb. 10:24). Christians are commanded to consider (pay attention to, be concerned for, look after) *someone* and *something*. The *someone* is "one another." The *something* is stirring up each other. What does this mean? The word translated "stir" can mean irritate, provoke, or even exasperate. It's used most frequently in a negative sense of provoking someone to anger or irritation. But, this is not the sense here. Instead, the writer of Hebrews is emphasizing an intentional provoking or promoting of "love and good works." This is another way of saying "godliness."

This makes sense when we think about life in the church. The church family is a collection of sinners who gather together to worship and grow more like Jesus. One tool that God uses for this is each other Christian in our lives. As we sense this role and intentionally consider how to provoke this godliness in our churches, we find ourselves "getting under each other's skin." Why? Because we are selfish. We don't like our flesh to be irritated—we want to be affirmed and left alone. But the church cannot do this. We love each other. We want to grow together in Christlikeness. Mere Christianity is very concerned with the church family. Our burden is for one another; we are our brother's and sister's keeper. The community that God provides around you serves you by scrubbing off the grimy build-up of self-orientation.

When you bring this full circle, you can see what the writer had in mind. It is the sinful isolation of the church's members that undermines this sanctifying process. If we don't gather, we can't "irritate" one another. Some gather but do so in a superficial way. Instead of stirring each other up, they simply chat up one another about a myriad of superficial things. There is nothing wrong with discussions about the weather, sports, politics, and other items. However, the church is called to be about something more weighty and valuable. We are about love and good works.

According to Hebrews, this is to be on everyone's radar and to-do list every day, and especially the Lord's Day when we gather. We are not meant to live the Christian life in isolation. And we can't do our jobs when we are being superficial. We can't serve God and others this way.

Unrealistic Expectations

As a pastor, I meet a lot of people who are looking for a church. One of the most helpful questions I can ask is "What are you looking for in a church?" In one sense I hate this question, because of the way it can reinforce a consumer mind-set. At the same time, it gets right to the point. People are looking for something. Then there's the other side of the spectrum, people who leave a church. I ask them the back door version of the front door question: "What were you unhappy about in this church?"

I have found that most people filter what they are looking for in a church not through the Bible as much as through their previous experiences or personal ideals. Some of the most common things I've heard and seen in the last ten years of pastoral ministry include the following desires:

- *Best friends*. People are looking for other people with whom they have a lot in common.
- *Youth ministry*. People are looking for the church to provide a Christian network of friends for their teenage kids.
- *Children's programs*. People often look for the church to be the catalyst for family discipleship.
- *Mercy ministry*. Some people want to be a part of a ministry to meet the physical needs of the community.
- *Music*. People look for a particular kind of musical experience during the singing time of a service.

Let me be clear: these are all good things. But what if none of these things is actually the church's primary job? If these things top the lists of what people are looking for, are they expecting both far too much and far too little from the church? The church's job is to preach, teach, and apply the Bible. We are to be faithful in preaching, discipleship, evangelism, and service. But there are no directives in the Bible for various programs for children or certain types of music. Though none of these interests are bad, we should be careful not to place greater emphasis on them than the Scriptures do.

Consider the pursuit of good friends at church. It is very good to have close friends, particularly from your fellowship. In fact, most of my closest friends are from our church family. But how do we pursue them? What is the basis for making friends? How are friendship sustained? Many people think of friendships as relationships in which people have a lot in common. And some people will leave a church saying, "I can't find people I have a lot in common with." This is a staggering and revealing statement. It is dangerously close to saying, "There are no Christians here," or "I am not a Christian," or "I don't value my identity as a Christian enough to consider it a basis for relationships."

Our identity as Christians provides our chief common feature and basis for friendship with other believers. You have the most important things in common with other Christians. You have the same story (saved from sin and death), passion (the glory of Christ), struggles (sin), hope (coming kingdom), authority (the Word of God), and so on. There is so much in common here! The problem is that we often promote worldly things to the position that only the gospel should hold. Then we wonder why the church cannot deliver. In fact, she should not deliver on worldly pursuits.

I am convinced that many professing Christians are simultaneously expecting too much and too little from the church. We are now in something of a "tail wagging the dog" scenario. Church leaders accommodate expectations of church shoppers. If one church won't meet their preferences, they can go to another. This becomes a significant long-term problem.

The church's role is really quite simple: to make and train disciples. If we do this, we will create a culture where friendships grow out of the gospel rather than in spite of it. Other programs will see their rightful place in the life of the Christian. As Christians we should all work together to raise the gospel flag above the other markers of identity.

Mission Drift

When we think of something as important as the church, the costs of deviation from God's design are great. After all, lives depend on faithfulness to God's Word. As we have already seen in this chapter, our conformity to Christ as believers hinges on what we do with the Bible. If we are off on the Word, then we will be off in people's lives. It is the gospel that has the power to save and sanctify.

Mission drift has become a popular phrase to capture subtle shifts from the church's priorities. These small and often imperceptible shifts happen over time and don't seem like much of a concern. However, after some time the church has wandered significantly off course.

This became clear to me in a meeting with a local megachurch pastor. Through a couple of mutual acquaintances I was able to sit down with this very popular pastor. After some small talk, I asked if we might talk about ministry. I said that I had a perception of his church from the outside looking in and wanted to get his insight. He obliged and we were off to the races. I asked him if he thought their ministry model was governed by pragmatism. His reply was unflinching, "Oh, absolutely." He went on to tell me that they would do just about anything to get people to come to church so they would meet Jesus. I also asked him about Bible teaching. He said it was secondary to people meeting Jesus. In fact, he said that he routinely sends people who want doctrine to our church. After thanking him, I asked him why. Again, he doubled down on people meeting and knowing Jesus.

I am absolutely in favor of evangelism, but I also see the importance of the church being equipped to know and apply God's Word. Far from being an evangelical cussword, *doctrine* refers to the very nutrients for the growth of the church in Christlikeness. Paul uses *doctrine* and its several synonyms to speak positively of essential content a pastor should be giving his people. In 2 Timothy we read of the inspiration of the *Scripture* (3:16), the priority of preaching *the* Word (4:2), persevering in *teaching* . . . or *doctrine* (4:3), and maintaining the *truth* (4:3–4). I don't know how to biblically rationalize a ministry that consciously avoids the teaching of doctrine. What is Christianity about if it is not about teaching and living its doctrine? How are Christians going to grow and learn contentment apart from learning the Bible?

These questions were chalked up as minor "differences." And since the popular pastor's church was ten times as large as the one where I pastor, he seemed quite comfortable in his approach. As I listened to him and considered the conversation later, I was struck by the subtle shifts over time. This megachurch was founded as a body that emphasized preaching and discipleship. Small drifts in mission, over time, led to a surprisingly radical departure from that emphasis. Now the congregation was crinkling its nose at such priorities.

When we think about the churches we belong to, we have to remember that what we believe dictates where we are going. This is why the apostle Paul was so adamant that the Galatians reject (or fire) any pastor who is not preaching the truth of God's Word (Gal. 1:6). As church members we have to remember that lives—contented lives—depend upon clear biblical teaching. Without a faithful church, you will not likely find content people.

‒ ‒ ‒

I have tried to be simple and clear about the importance of the local church in God's purpose to fasten our hearts upon Christ. Integral to this divine purpose for the church is the faithful teaching and receiving of the Word of God. As we are equipped, we grow more and more like Christ. There are plenty of reasons why we might find ourselves discontent with a church or the people in the church; we are a congregation of sinners, after all. However, let's not lose sight of this fact that if the Word of God is faithfully taught and the congregation is pursuing holiness, this church is serving you very well. There may be more things that churches can do, but there is nothing better than this. Being content with your local church means that you have embraced her mission and celebrated her faithfulness.

Review Questions

1. Have you been guilty of being a little embarrassed by your "ordinary" church?

2. What is the church's role in making God's people content in him?

3. How does the church "assure" and "deter"?

4. What are some ways in which we can undermine the local church's work in our own lives?

5. What is the bottom-line criterion for evaluating whether or not a church is serving its people?

You Are Not Yet Home

"Are we there yet?" We hadn't even gotten onto the highway when our four-year-old son uttered these infamous words. The worst part was that he was serious. As we continued on the first of three days of driving, the inquiries bubbled up from the middle row of the minivan. In his mind he was on vacation. He may have been in Omaha, Nebraska, but in his excitement he already had a toe in the ocean. After being packed up in his seat and pumped up with anticipation by stories from his big brothers and sisters, he was not prepared to wait. So the status updates continued as we plodded along.

How do parents handle this situation? They usually start by explaining that the trip is going to take some time while reassuring children that they are in fact going to the beach. Perhaps parents entertain the kids with stories from previous trips or specific plans of fun things to do. But even as parents and older siblings do this, they themselves begin to get restless. Thinking about the ocean can heighten the longing all the more.

So when you stop for gas or food, it's usually helpful to stretch your legs and let the kids run around a bit, but only for a brief break. You are on a schedule, after all! You wouldn't think of just staying at the rest stop. Everyone is intent on getting where you're going. Your shared restlessness produces a hearty resolve. You might even say that you're not fully happy until you get there.

As Christians we often experience discontentment by forgetting that we're not "there" yet. We are moving ahead to our destination and must not settle at the rest stop. To forget our true journey's end would leave us in a disappointing place. But in this ultimate road trip to our new home, God is leading us to a new city. He has given us a taste of this new world through the Holy Spirit. We have these precious promises laid before us to remind us that we are not yet home. Knowing that we are passing through and where we are going allows us to be content in the world. We are like pilgrims making our way to another land.

We Are Pilgrims

Earlier we looked at Hebrews 13, where God reminds his people that they are to be content with what he has given them rather than grumbling, coveting, and worrying: "Keep your life free from love of money, and be content with what you have, for he has said, 'I will never leave you nor forsake you'" (13:5). You'll notice that the writer references something that God has said elsewhere in his Word. The quoted passage is Joshua 1:5. Joshua was preparing to lead the Israelites to the Promised Land. The sustaining truth for these believers in their wilderness walk was the fact that God would not leave them.

The writer of Hebrews, seizing upon the historical narrative, makes his point about contentment. Likening our Christian experience to a journey through the wilderness, he urges believers to be content with what they have. This recapitulation of the believer's journey to the Promised Land is a regular theme in Hebrews.[1] The writer calls our destination "rest" (4:11), "a city" that God has built, "a better country . . . a heavenly one" (11:16), "the heavenly

---

1. See Hebrews 3, where we are called to learn from the downfall of those who have gone before us, those who heard the word of God but did not have faith.

Jerusalem" (12:22), "heaven" (12:23), "a kingdom" (12:28), and "the city that is to come" (13:14).

As we believers are marching resolutely toward our heavenly country, God is with us and protects us. Quoting from a couple of familiar psalms,[2] the writer of Hebrews continues,

So we can confidently say,

"The Lord is my helper;
   I will not fear;
what can man do to me?" (13:6)

We are not left alone as pilgrims. As we go on in faith, God goes on with us. Learning from the errors of the many faithless Israelites, we are reminded to continue in faith, that we may enter that rest (Heb. 4:11).

We Have a Dual Citizenship

With such an emphasis on where we are going, an objection may be leveled, "Do Christians live in an ethereal world detached from the pressing realities of everyday life?" Definitely not! We have work to do here. Simon Kistemaker comments:

Christians are to be "the salt of the earth" and "the light of the world" (Matt. 5:13–14). Wherever God in his providence has placed them, they are to be Christ's ambassadors (2 Cor. 5:20). They are to represent Christ by boldly speaking the Word he has given them. Yet they know the brevity of life and the fleeting nature of this world. Therefore, they look and long for their eternal dwelling: "a city that is to come."[3]

This definitely presents a tension. We are to be living faithfully now—trusting in God's promises, resting in God himself—while

---

2. Psalms 118 and 56.
3. Simon J. Kistemaker, *Exposition of the Epistle to the Hebrews*, New Testament Commentary (Grand Rapids, MI: Baker, 1984), 422–23.

looking ahead to where we are going. In his letter to the Philippian church the apostle Paul reminded his readers of the believer's
ultimate loyalty and longing: "But our citizenship is in heaven,
and from it we await a Savior, the Lord Jesus Christ, who will
transform our lowly body to be like his glorious body, by the
power that enables him even to subject all things to himself" (Phil.
3:20–21). Here we can see both the loyalty (our citizenship is in
heaven) and the longing (we await our coming Savior) that mark
our dual citizenship. We are citizens of heaven, and we live here as
citizens of this world. Far from living detached and unimportant
lives, Christians embrace lives formed by the gospel and characterized by faith, hope, and love. Ralph Martin explains:

> The apostle here indicates the double allegiance of the Philip-
> pian Christians. As Roman subjects they are citizens of the
> far distant, capital city of Rome, where the emperor has his
> residence. As servants of "another king, one called Jesus"
> (Acts 17:7), they are citizens of that capital city, where the
> King of kings has his domicile, and whose advent to establish
> his reign on this earth and to rescue his people (1 Thess. 1:10)
> is awaited. Here on earth, meanwhile, they are resident aliens
> who dwell temporarily in a foreign country, but have their
> citizenship elsewhere.[4]

Like Christian in Bunyan's classic *The Pilgrim's Progress*, we are
passing through, making our way to the Celestial City.

This dual citizenship informs our identity; it shows our orientation. In the same section of Philippians 3, Paul contrasts true
and false worship by showing that there are those whose "god
is their belly, and they glory in their shame, with minds set on
earthly things" (3:19). The natural religious disposition of humanity is orientated around this world. It is no surprise, then, that at
the very center of their being, "where their life finds its direction,

---

4. Ralph P. Martin, *Philippians: An Introduction and Commentary*, Tyndale New Testament Commentaries 11 (Downers Grove, IL: InterVarsity Press, 1987), 167.

where attitudes and tendencies are fashioned which subsequently influence decisions and govern likes and dislikes—at this vital centre the world and its ways are the whole object of attention," says J. A. Motyer. "The mind is set upon earth."[5] In contrast to this, says Paul, we are citizens of heaven. In fact, our minds and our affections are calibrated by heaven's King, the Lord Jesus Christ. We are awaiting his return even as we aim to live faithfully for him.

Contentment in God Is Characteristic of This Dual Citizenship

After drawing this key distinction about our identity and orientation, Paul makes a startling statement in the next chapter: "I can do all things through him who strengthens me" (Phil. 4:13). Often this verse is torn from its context and its meaning is inflated. It becomes a blank check for whatever we want. But as Nathan Busenitz points out:

> The irony is that, by taking this verse *out* of context, many people have actually turned it on its head—making it mean the opposite of what it actually means. They have turned it into a slogan of personal empowerment—a declaration of self-achievement, ambition, and accomplishment. For many, this verse has been trivialized into some sort of motivating motto for material prosperity, career advancement, or athletic success.[6]

However, the context of the passage is about contentment. The verse is not about everything going well but about trusting God when things don't go well. It's not about being rich and happy but about being content whether you are rich or poor. In other words, what is so striking about Philippians 4:13 is not that we can achieve everything we wish for but that God enables self-centered

---

5. J. A. Motyer, *The Message of Philippians*, The Bible Speaks Today (Downers Grove, IL: InterVarsity Press, 1984), 188.
6. Nathan Busenitz, "I Can Do All Things," *The Cripplegate*, October 27, 2011, http://thecripplegate.com/i-can-do-all-things.

people to find their identity, joy, and purpose in him rather than themselves. In all that we do, he makes us content in him.

Circumstances That Unsettle Us

We are well aware of times when we find ourselves unsettled and knocked a bit off balance. Like a rush of dizziness when we get up too quickly, rapidly changing circumstances can leave us reaching for something stable. This is when our dual citizenship can refresh and remind us of who we are and where we are going. There is a reorienting stability in the truth that we are not yet home. Let me highlight a number of situations and show how we can find our way back to contentment by remembering the truth that we are not home.

The Sting of Broken Relationships

Few things are more painful than having a meaningful relationship broken. When we've formed close personal bonds with people, the sting is particularly acute. Sadly, even in the church Christians experience this sting. This is especially troubling because two important requirements for membership are acknowledging personal sin and humbly seeking peace and unity. Our gospel-informed expectations of the church can make the reality of broken relationships with other Christians notably unsettling.

We must remember that we are not the first to experience this. David knew this firsthand.

> For it is not an enemy who taunts me—
>   then I could bear it;
> it is not an adversary who deals insolently with me—
>   then I could hide from him.
> But it is you, a man, my equal,
>   my companion, my familiar friend.
> We used to take sweet counsel together;
>   within God's house we walked in the throng.
>   (Ps. 55:12–14)

It was also true of the greater David, Jesus Christ. Remember, our Lord was betrayed by one of his own disciples, and his family thought he was mad. We are certainly not promised a better reception than our Lord received, and we should not be surprised when we encounter divisions.

We must also remember that we are heading to a place where there will be no more painful breaches and all past hurts will be properly healed. The hymn "Ten Thousand Times Ten Thousand" captures it well:

> O then what raptured greetings
> On Canaan's happy shore;
> What knitting severed friendships up,
> Where partings are no more!
> Then eyes with joy shall sparkle,
> That brimmed with tears of late;
> Orphans no longer fatherless,
> Nor widows desolate.[7]

When the sting of broken relationships unsettles us, we can remember what Christ went through and where he is taking us. He is taking his people to a new city where all things—even relationships—are restored.

Being Falsely Accused

A friend of mine witnessed some questionable business practices by his coworkers. As he probed deeper, he found things that made him very uncomfortable and felt that he must address the issue. As it happened, the web of corruption was widespread, and the overall impact was even greater than he had expected. In an effort to save face and discredit my friend, the guilty parties began to falsely accuse him. He knew what was true, and he knew he was doing the right thing. Yet he found himself on the receiving end of false accusations that jeopardized his reputation and career.

---

7. Henry Alford, "Ten Thousand Times Ten Thousand," 1867.

As I discussed this with my friend, I found him remarkably content. He shared with me that he knew what was true and that the Lord would use this ordeal for good. Then he reminded me that this world is not his home. While this type of trouble grieves him, he expects it. The world is fallen. It makes heaven all the more sweet.

A healthy doctrine of God's providence framed in by the reality of the coming kingdom can be like spiritual rebar in our souls. Like roads that experience wear, tear and even cracking, our lives show the weathering of this cursed world. But with fortified minds and hearts fortified by unbending truth, we are able to rest in God and even grow in the midst of trials.

The Death of a Loved One

When we give ourselves in love to other people, we are bonded to them. We enjoy a closeness, an intimacy, when we love. When a loved one dies, we feel this attachment in the opposite way. Grieving is the expression of love's closeness interrupted. It hurts deeply to no longer share life with those we love.

As a pastor I have counseled many grieving families after the death of their loved ones. People find respite and joy amid the grief in many different ways. Stories, pictures, visiting familiar sites, and reading old letters often refresh people. However, all of these are momentary reprieves for grief. The one thing that upholds a grieving family member like a sturdy banister is the hope of the resurrection. In the midst of pain of loss that crowds out other concerns, the only truth that I have seen provide enduring comfort and enable people to stand is the true hope that Christ brings. The apostle Peter puts it this way:

> Blessed be the God and Father of our Lord Jesus Christ! According to his great mercy, he has caused us to be born again to a living hope through the resurrection of Jesus Christ from the dead, to an inheritance that is imperishable, undefiled,

and unfading, kept in heaven for you, who by God's power are being guarded through faith for a salvation ready to be revealed in the last time. In this you rejoice, though now for a little while, if necessary, you have been grieved by various trials. (1 Pet. 1:3–6)

This hope is not simply hope in hope. Rather, it is hope anchored in a person. In other words, hope is as good as its object. And in our case, our hope is anchored in the unchanging, infinitely powerful, truth-telling God of the Bible!

Chronic Sickness

A number of people in our churches suffer from chronic sickness or disease. Some are afflicted in more visible ways than others, but many suffer greatly. The need for contentment brings unique challenges for these dear brothers and sisters. And those with little to no hope for recovery can find themselves tempted to depression or despair.

The causes for despair are often loneliness and hopelessness, not the suffering itself. As believers we know that we are never alone (Matt. 28:19–20); in fact, we have a merciful High Priest who is able to sympathize with us in our weakness (Heb. 4:14–15). What's more, God has surrounded us with believers in a local church to help bear our burdens (Gal. 6:1–2) and encourage us in our Christian lives (Heb. 3:13). So, even when we are weak, we are never hopeless as Christians. We are trusting in the Savior, who has conquered sin, Satan, and death. He is bringing restoration to all things. When we think about the miracles in the Gospel narratives, we are reminded that Jesus has the power to heal the symptoms of the curse of sin *and* to remove the curse altogether.[8]

We forget this, though, don't we? Although we remember that

8. This seems to be the point of Mark 2, where Jesus says, "'Which is easier, to say to the paralytic, "Your sins are forgiven," or to say, "Rise, take up your bed and walk"? But that you may know that the Son of Man has authority on earth to forgive sins'—he said to the paralytic—'I say to you, rise, pick up your bed, and go home'" (Mark 2:9–11).

he has the power to remove the penalty of sin, we forget that he also is reconciling all things to himself (Col. 1:20). This means that he is going to vanquish every trace of the curse when all things are made new. The crippled man will leap, the mute will sing, the weak will be strong, the quadriplegic will dance, cancer will be gone, and Christ will be enveloped in praise.

In J. R. R. Tolkien's *The Return of the King*, Sam Gamgee asks, "Is everything sad going to come untrue?" Indeed it will.[9] When we look at the end through the lenses of the gospel, we have reason not only to be hopeful but even to be learning contentment in the midst of our trials.

The Moral Revolution

As I write this, our society is in the midst of a moral revolution. Marriage is being redefined, while religious liberty seems to be evaporating. Many Christians feel they've had the wind knocked out of them. This was acutely felt after the 2015 US Supreme Court decision that extended to same-sex couples the fundamental right to marry. Any morning fog of lingering impressions that our nation is neutral toward biblical Christianity was blown away by celebrations that included the White House lit up in rainbow colors. At some point Christians looked up and said, "Hey, I'm no longer welcome here."

This realization is exactly right. This is not our home. For centuries Christians have lived in communities that did not welcome them, however they survived and the gospel thrived. Remember the words of the writer of Hebrews as he tried to encourage a community of believers feeling the pinch of the culture around them: "Here we have no lasting city, but we seek the city that is to come" (Heb. 13:14).

As Christians we have the responsibility (and privilege) to be greatly burdened for our neighbors (Matt. 9:35–37), jealous for

9. J. R. R. Tolkien, *The Lord of the Rings: 50th Anniversary, the Complete Classic in One Volume* (London: HarperCollins, 2005), 951.

our King (Matt. 6:9–10), and longing for the city to come (Heb. 13:14). Often this last one rattles our contentment. Even through this moral revolution, God is gracious to lift our eyes above the headlines to see the promised gates of the Celestial City. Here we have no abiding city. Everything here has an expiration date; it is only a matter of time before it is gone.

We have to remember this as Christians living in the West (or anywhere else in the world). While I may have a physical address where I lay my head at night, I am not home, because we as Christians seek the city that is to come. This seeking is an ongoing, intentional pursuit. It is to characterize our lives and fuel our contentment. We are looking ahead to the city that will come down from heaven where we will dwell with God and all his blood-bought saints forever! There will be no feelings of being unwelcome there when we are gathered round the great table to enjoy feasting and fellowship with the church. Christ will be there, ruling and reigning with all his people giving themselves to him freely (Revelation 21–22).

In a strange twist of providence, the moral revolution that knocks the wind out of us can also serve to put wind in our sails. By making us feel like we are not home, it reminds us of our true home. What a surprising providence and lesson in the school of contentment!

The Prosperity of the Wicked

It is a perennial temptation to become discontent when things are not going as well as we might prefer, but this becomes more pronounced when we see unbelievers seemingly doing better than we are. Something seems to be off in our salvation equation. They don't love God, but they appear to be doing great. I love God, and my life is much harder.

This is not a new temptation for believers. The psalmist wrote,

> For I was envious of the arrogant
> when I saw the prosperity of the wicked. (Ps. 73:3)

In fact, he says that this observation was such a temptation that he almost slipped himself.

Certainly you have felt this temptation as well. How do you deal with it? Perspective is key. Remember that as a believer you are simply passing through and are headed to the new and perfect city. But for an unbeliever this is everything. There is nothing better because there is nothing further. Friends, our response to seeing unbelievers prosper should not be envy but pity and compassion. This is all the heaven they will ever have, and this is all the hell you will ever have. Look ahead and interpret things in light of the end, and you will find yourself made more content even though you lack and others overflow. Yours is coming, and it will be more and far better than you could ever have envied here on earth!

Persecution

As we have seen, God often uses surprising means to loosen our grip on this world and refasten our grip on him. He takes away our comforts to make us take comfort in him. On occasion he uses persecution to bring this about. Persecution, in general terms, is opposition to believers and their message. It can be expressed mildly (dirty looks, rudeness, etc.) or more intensely (ostracizing, prison, or even death). Jesus told us to expect this; if the world persecuted him, it will persecute his followers (John 15:20). Peter, writing from the context of intense persecution, reminded fellow believers to not be surprised by the fiery trial that awaited them (1 Pet. 4:12). This is part of what it means to count the cost.

Peter's reminder is also grace. Doesn't this sound strange? It is grace because it reminds us of who we are and where we are going. When we are undergoing persecution, we are reminded of the aroma of grace. No matter how bad the suffering, we should remember it is never as great as our sin deserves. After all, if it were not for God's saving grace, we would not be receiving the stroke and might even be the ones giving it. Further, it reminds us of the age to come. Suffering is purposeful, and it produces glory (2 Cor. 4:17).

Persecution, then, whether mild or intense, serves as a refining work of grace. It reminds us of the gospel and it propels our hearts and minds toward Immanuel's land, where the gospel song will be on everyone's lips.

Personal Sin

Nothing unsettles us like our remaining indwelling sin. As Christians we have been saved from the *penalty* and *power* of sin but still wait for the day when the *presence* of sin is finally removed.

If the heart of discontent is a failure to trust and treasure God supremely, then the great desire for the one who is chasing contentment is to land with both feet in the heavenly Jerusalem, where sin is finally and forever removed!

Our struggles with sin, then, become a great reminder that in the end, it will all be removed. Christ has secured this by his atoning death on Calvary. We know as Christians that not only the broken world will be restored but we also—the broken people! This is part of the groaning wherewith we join the rest of creation. We are people who are most content in God but discontent in ourselves and our sin. We long to cross through the gates of the new city and praise God without hindrance, fully trusting and treasuring him.

Chase Contentment in Light of the End

What we are after as Christians is to fully embrace Christ and everything he has earned for us. Doing this displaces our discontentment and settles us upon him. To that end, I have found the following four practices immensely helpful on a daily basis.

Take a Look Around

Look around and see your brothers and sisters in Christ. See some struggling, and pray for them. See others doing well, and rejoice for them. Taking our eyes off ourselves and looking at others can remind us of how God is working in the lives of his people.

Take a Look Back

Do you remember what it was like before you came to Christ? Paul describes our former state as being without God and without hope in the world (Eph. 2:12). When the message of the gospel came to us and was united with faith, a new world was opened to us. It was like going from two-dimensional in black and white to three-dimensional in living color! God had truly opened our eyes and captivated our longings with his grace. We were taught to rest in him. Like looking at old wedding pictures, remember that day with all its excitement, hope, and joy. And then let it fuel contentment in the present, knowing that by God's grace you will endure until the end.

Take a Look Ahead

Much of this chapter has been looking ahead, so I urge you to continue doing this, even as you look back and around. Believer, this is not your home. You are headed to a new world where righteousness dwells and joys are yours forevermore (Ps. 16:11). Dwell much upon the coming kingdom.

Take a Look at Christ

It is a simple formula really: if you want to be content, think less about yourself and more about Christ. Robert Murray M'Cheyne said it well:

> "The heart is deceitful above all things, and desperately wicked: who can know it?" Jer. 17:9. Learn much of the Lord Jesus. For every look at yourself, take ten looks at Christ. He is altogether lovely. Such infinite majesty, and yet such meekness and grace, and all for sinners, even the chief! Live much in the smiles of God. Bask in his beams. Feel his all-seeing eye settled on you in love, and repose in his almighty arms. . . . Let your

soul be filled with a heart-ravishing sense of the sweetness and excellency of Christ and all that is in Him. Let the Holy Spirit fill every chamber of your heart; and so there will be no room for folly, or the world, or Satan, or the flesh.[10]

Looking upon Christ and the glorious promises that he has secured for you will bring you to a place of contentment. Charles Spurgeon makes this point with vivid contrast:

> The Christian is the most contented man in the world, but he is the least contented with the world. He is like a traveller in an inn, perfectly satisfied with the inn and its accommodation, considering it as an inn, but putting quite out of all consideration the idea of making it his home. He baits by the way, and is thankful, but his desires lead him ever onward towards that better country where the many mansions are prepared. The believer is like a man in a sailing vessel, well content with the good ship for what it is, and hopeful that it may bear him safely across the sea, willing to put up with all its inconveniences without complaint; but if you ask him whether he would choose to live on board in that narrow cabin, he will tell you that he longs for the time when the harbour shall be in view, and the green fields, and the happy homesteads of his native land. We, my brethren, thank God for all the appointments of providence; whether our portion be large or scant we are content because God has appointed it: yet our portion is not here, nor would we have it here if we might![11]

Are we there yet? Absolutely not. But we soon shall be!

Review Questions

1. Do you feel restless here, or are you longing for another land?

2. How does our dual citizenship as Christians orient our pursuit?

10. Robert Murray M'Cheyne and Andrew A. Bonar, *Memoir and Remains of Robert Murray M'Cheyne* (Edinburgh: Banner of Truth, 1973), 293.
11. Charles Spurgeon, "The Glorious Hereafter and Ourselves," accessed March 29, 2016, http://www.spurgeongems.org/vols16-18/chs912.pdf.

3. A verse like Philippians 4:13 is often used in ways that seem to undermine its context and plain meaning. What does "I can do all things through him who strengthens me" have to do with contentment?

4. How has God used pain, suffering, and discouragement in your life to make you long for heaven?

5. How do we chase contentment in light of the end?

Conclusion

At its simplest, *gospel* means good news. When you first become a Christian, that good news is taken in manageable bites. You learn that you are forgiven by God because of Christ's sacrificial death on the cross. As you grow, the gospel doesn't change, but your perspective on it and appreciation for it does. You learn that you have been adopted, rescued, redeemed, and reconciled. You learn that you have been loved, even before the foundation of the world. You come to see in greater detail that the doing and dying of Jesus truly is your basis for joy. As Tim Keller has rightly observed, "The gospel is not just the A-B-C's of but the A-Z of Christianity. The gospel is not just the minimum required doctrine necessary to enter the kingdom, but the way we make real progress in the kingdom."[1]

In this book we have seen how practical this statement truly is. Through the gospel God lovingly accomplishes and applies redemption for people who have sought happiness in something other than him. Humanity has all turned aside and served the creation rather than the Creator. Instead of leaving us hungry and hurting in our rebellion, God acts. He pursues us. He comes after us. And to what end? It is so that through this gracious rescue we might find ourselves agreeing with him about his all-surpassing

---

1. Erik Raymond, "Keller: You Never Get beyond the Gospel," *TGC* (*The Gospel Coalition*), September 9, 2009, https://blogs.thegospelcoalition.org/erikraymond/2009/09/09/keller-you-never-get-beyond-the-gospel.

supremacy and sufficiency. Through the gospel, God makes himself our treasure. In other words, God makes us content in him.

We know that this contentment is not simply idealistic but rather characteristic of the Christian life. As believers we continue to learn contentment by learning to trust and treasure God in every situation. God has provided us with the Bible and the church to be the means by which we work this out in our lives. As believers we draw near to the throne of grace so that we may receive mercy and find grace to help us in times of need (Heb. 4:16). This help is never less than recalibrating our hearts and minds to the truth of the gospel. We ask God to make us content in him and to help us to see through the shiny wrappers around us. We have who we need, we have what we need, and we are going where we need to go. Therefore, we plead with God that we might truly trust and treasure Jesus Christ.

In his book *The Art of Divine Contentment*, Thomas Watson described five characteristics of a contented heart.[2] With our course marked out for learning contentment, let's think about how we might evaluate where we are in our own personal progress.

A Contented Spirit Is a Silent Spirit

The one who is content is not complaining against God; he does not grumble and murmur. Watson observes:

> When Samuel tells Eli that heavy message from God, that he would "judge his house, and that the iniquity of his family should not be purged away with sacrifice forever," (1 Sam. 3:13–14) doth Eli murmur or dispute? No, he hath not one word to say against God: "it is the Lord, let him do what seemeth him good." On the other hand, Pharaoh, one who did not know God and therefore was discontent said, "who is the Lord? why should I suffer all this? why should I be brought into this low condition? who is the Lord?"

---

2. Thomas Watson, *The Art of Divine Contentment: An Exposition of Philippians 4:11*, chap. 13, accessed April 1, 2016, http://www.biblebb.com/files/TW/tw-contentment.htm. Subsequent quotations from Watson are also drawn from chap. 13.

Remember well the distinction between complaining *to* God and complaining *about* God. When we complain to God, we are bringing our problems and vices and crying out to God for wisdom, grace, and help. When we are complaining about God, we are attacking his character. This is ungodliness at its core. When Aaron's sons were judged and killed, he "held his peace" (Lev. 10:3). He was silent. However, when Jonah was grumbling before God, God asked him, "Do you do well to be angry?" (Jonah 4:4). The difference is clear. Silence is a reflection of peaceful trust—even amid circumstances that are difficult to understand. Anger, grumbling, and complaining represent inner turmoil and a lack of trust in God.

How would others describe you? Are you apt to speak out and give vent to your frustrations with others and God? Or are you inclined to hold your peace and see the Lord in the situation?

A Contented Spirit Is a Cheerful Spirit

Contentment is more than patience (though it is not less). It involves a cheerfulness of the soul. Watson says, "A contented Christian is more than passive; he doth not only bear the cross, but take up the cross." This is why Paul can be sorrowful yet always rejoicing (2 Cor. 6:10). He can be content in his sufferings even when they are so difficult (2 Cor. 12:10). He doesn't just say, "The will of the Lord be done"; he says, "Rejoice in the Lord always; again I will say, rejoice" (Phil. 4:4). Watson rightly quips, "'God loveth a cheerful giver' . . . and God loves a cheerful liver." When we are content with our lot in Christ, we have the ground of cheerfulness within us. We carry our pardon sealed in our very hearts. Could you be accused of being cheerful, even amid difficulty?

A Contented Spirit Is a Thankful Spirit

Scripture reminds us to give thanks in everything (1 Thess. 5:18). When we are content, we spy mercy in every condition and have our hearts laminated with thanksgiving. Anyone can thank God for prosperity, but the contented person blesses him when afflicted (2 Cor. 6:10; Phil. 4:9–11). The discontented heart is ever complaining of its current condition, but the contented spirit is always thanking God for it. Watson says, "A contented heart is a temple where the praises of God are sung forth, not a sepulcher wherein they are buried." Even while encountering a season of intense difficulty, the contented person may still—because contentment is a work of grace from the inside out—have his or her heart dilated in thankfulness. "There is always gratulatory music in a contented soul; the Spirit of grace works in the heart like new wine, which under the heaviest pressures of sorrow will have a vent open for thankfulness: this is to be content." Are you characteristically thankful?

A Contented Spirit Is Not Bound by Circumstances

Because contentment works from the inside out, it is shielded from the ever-changing circumstances outside us. Remember, Paul himself said that his contentment was seen "in any and every circumstance" (Phil. 4:12). Do you find yourself content when things are going well but struggling when the winds are contrary?

A Contented Spirit Will Not Avoid Trouble by Means of Sin

Resting in God's providence does not mean that we stand still. Contentment does not mean complacency. However, when there is something we should pursue, but God's timing has not yet made it available, a contented spirit does not rush ahead anyway. The discontented will not wait. Watson explains that if God does not open the door of his providence, "they will break it open and wind themselves out of affliction by sin; bringing their souls into trouble; this is far from holy contentment, this is unbelief broken into rebellion." Contentment would rather wait upon God than sin against God. "A contented Christian is willing to wait God's leisure, and will not stir till God open a door." The spirit of contentment says, "I would rather stay in prison than purchase liberty by sinning against God." Watson punctuates this point well:

> A contented Christian will not remove, till as the Israelites he sees a pillar of cloud and fire going before him. "It is good that a man should both hope, and quietly wait for the salvation of the Lord." (La. 3. 26) It is good to stay God's leisure and not to extricate ourselves out of trouble, till we see the star of God's providence pointing out a way to us.

– – –

We end this book where we began, considering words from previous ages about contentment in God. Is it a lost art? Of course not. Contentment is gospel art, crafted by the Holy Spirit in the lives of Christ's people. Ever since the garden of Eden the world has been discontent, and ever since then God has been pursuing people to make them content in him. We have the privilege of not only knowing this but experiencing it first hand.

General Index

"Abide with Me" (hymn), 125
accountability, 139
Adam and Eve
    commission of, 133
    God's pursuit of, 42–43
    lured into sin, 81–83
    sin of, 40–41
afflictions, 113, 121–23
applications of text, 74
assure and deter, 135–36
Augustine, 77

Beeke, Joel, 77
Berry, Wendell, 84
best friends, 141
Bible reading, 71–75
bitterness, 27, 126
Bliss, Philip, 105–6
Brady, Tom, 21–22
broken relationships, 151–52
brushing teeth, 136–37
Bunyan, John, 149
Burroughs, Jeremiah, 16–17,
    26–27, 30–31, 101, 116, 119
Busenitz, Nathan, 150
busyness, 27

Calvin, John, 66, 69–70, 76–78
Chalmers, Thomas, 46
cheerful spirit, 164
children's ministry, 141
Christian biographies, 14

Christian life, goal of, 65
Christlikeness, 140
chronic sickness, 154–55
church
    as bride of Christ, 130
    and contentment, 129, 134–44
    importance of, 130, 135–36
    as ordinary, 136–37
church shoppers, 142
circumstances
    and contentment, 12, 25, 151,
        165
    and desires, 109–10
    and providence, 116
citizenship in heaven, 149
complacency, 165
complaining, to God or at God, 26,
    164
contentment
    as the "Amen" of joy, 12, 46
    and the church, 129, 134–44
    and circumstances, 12, 25, 151,
        165
    definition of, 23
    as elusive, 35, 38–42
    with God, 12, 65–68, 104
    and the gospel, 52
    as inward and spiritual, 92
    and providence, 114–15, 121,
        125
    as work of grace, 27–29

conversion, as pledging supreme loyalty to God, 45
coveting, 92–93, 102–3
Cowper, William, 11, 124
cross of Christ, 127

daily bread, 108
Daniel, 123
David, 123
death
   of loved one, 153–54
   reality of, 109
dental-chair devotions, 71, 75, 78
desires, and circumstances, 109–10
desires of the eyes, 92–93
desires of the flesh, 90–91
Dever, Mark, 62
discipleship culture, in the church, 138–39
discontentment, 22, 27, 125–26, 147
   from false promises, 95
   as Great Commission of world, flesh, and Devil, 85–86
distraction, 27
doctrine, 143
dual citizenship, 148–50, 151

Edwards, Jonathan, 46
emptiness of riches, 68
enticing, 89
Esau, 92
evangelism, 143

faithfulness, impediments to, 139–44
false accusation, 152–53
fear of missing out (FOMO), 22
Ferguson, Sinclair, 47–48
flesh, 91, 108

glorifying and enjoying God, 65
God
   as eternal, 36
   glory of, 37

as good, 116–17, 127
independence of, 36
as love, 36–37
love of, 39
as powerful, 117
rescues his hungry, hurting people, 44
as source of contentment, 104
sovereignty of, 114, 127
as unchanging, 36
will not forsake his people, 125
wisdom of, 117–18, 127
godliness, 65–68, 140
"God Moves in a Mysterious Way" (hymn), 11, 124
gospel
   and contentment, 52
   as good news, 162
grace and contentment, 27–29
Griffin, Hayne, 67
grumbling, 26–27, 116, 125, 163

"Hallelujah! What a Savior!" (hymn), 105–6
heaven, free from weight of sin, 107
Heidelberg Catechism, 29, 113–14
Helm, David, 138
Henry, Matthew, 69
High Priestly Prayer, 45
holiness, 68
Holy Spirit resides in us, 48
hope, 77
hospitality, 139
humility, 76, 110

"I Asked the Lord" (hymn), 122–23
image of God, 38, 101
inward versus outward contentment, 30–31
IOUS (prayer acronym), 72, 78
isolation, from the church, 139–40
Israel
   grumbling and complaining of, 116

wilderness wandering of, 136, 147

Jesus Christ
death of, 105–6, 108
incarnation of, 105, 108
as last Adam, 133–34
obedience of, 105
self-denial of, 110
Joseph, 29–30, 123
joy in knowing God, 45–46

Keller, Tim, 77–78, 162
Kistemaker, Simon, 148
knowing Christ, 47–48
knowledge of God and self, 52

"law work," 60–61
Lea, Thomas, 67
learning contentment, 15
Lewis, C. S., 35, 87
life as short, 109
London Baptist Confession of Faith, 114n3
looking ahead, 159
looking at Christ, 159–60
looking back, 159
"love and good works," 140
loving creation more than God, 41
lures of temptation, 89, 90–94
lust, 90–91
Luther, Martin, 77

M'Cheyne, Robert Murray, 159–60
marriage, redefinition of, 155
Martin, Ralph, 149
meditation on Word of God, 72–75
megachurches, 143–44
mercy, 56–57, 60–61, 62, 123–24
mercy ministry, 141
military analogy, 64–65
mission drift, in the church, 142–44
mistakes, sin relativized as, 56
moderation of delights, 109
moral revolution, 155–56

mortification of sin, 109
Motyer, J. A., 150
murmur, 163
music, in the church, 141

Newton, John, 122–23

obedience to God, 88
O'Brien, Peter, 134
"one another" passages, 138–39
ordinary, church as, 130, 136–37
Owen, John, 59–60, 87–88

passions, 92
Paul
pursuit of contentment, 15, 54–55
sense of depravity, 55
Paul and Silas, imprisonment of, 23–24
persecution, 157–58
perseverance through trials, 61–62
personality cults, in the church, 131
pilgrims, Christians as, 147–48
Piper, John, 72
possessions, 93–94
pragmatism, 143
prayer, 72, 75–77
pride, 57–58
pride of life, 93–94
Prodigal Son, 44
prosperity, 165
providence, 113
and contentment, 114–15, 121, 125
as purposeful, 118–21
resting in, 29–32, 126–28

quiet, of contentment, 25–27, 29

reading Scripture aloud, 73–74
Reagan, Nancy, 97
Regan, Brian, 94
rejoicing, over restoration of lost, 44
repentance, 76

resting in providence, 126–28, 165
restlessness, 35, 127
reverence for God, 76
rules, 39

sanctification, 60, 135
Sanders, Fred, 36, 37
Satan
    as god of this world, 85, 94
    lures Adam and Eve into sin,
        81–83
    seasons of blessing and affliction,
        113
seed of the woman, 43–44
self-centered, 100
self-denial, 98–101, 103–4, 107–10
self-esteem, 103
self-indulgence, 108
selfishness, 104, 127
self-sufficiency, 58, 103
silence of contentment, 163–64
sin, 53, 58–59
    as against God, 53
    as certain and severe, 54
    contented spirit fights against,
        165–66
    as expression of discontentment,
        98
    indwelling, 158
    Paul on, 55
    as pervasive, 42, 53
    relativizing of, 56
    slaves of righteousness, 108–9
    slaves of sin, 108
Smethurst, Matt, 85
social media, 22
Socrates, 28
spiritual blindness, 52
Spurgeon, Charles, 160

Stoicism, 67
Stott, John, 66
suffering, 154–55, 157–58
sufficiency in Christ, 47–48, 58

temptation, 87–94
"Ten Thousand Times Ten Thou-
    sand" (hymn), 152
thanksgiving, 164–65
Tolkien, J. R. R., 155
treasuring Christ, 74
trials, 61–62, 121–23
Trinity, 35–36, 45
trust in God, 76, 110

union with Christ, 47
unrealistic expectations, toward the
    church, 140–42

voicing complaints to God, 26

Watson, Thomas, 16–17, 108, 109,
    163–66
weakness, as qualification for the
    kingdom, 58
Westminster Shorter Catechism, 65
Whitney, Don, 73
wicked, prosperity of, 156–57
Winslow, Octavius, 106–7
Word, forms and transforms Chris-
    tians, 69–71
world, in rebellion against God,
    84–85
worldliness, 27
worldly joys, 46
worldly things, in the church, 142
worry, 126

youth ministry, 141

Scripture Index

Genesis
1 119
1:1 . . . . 35, 36
1:26–28 38
1:28 133
1:28–31 . . . . 39, 40
2:15 133
2:17 40
3 . . . . 40, 45, 87, 89, 108, 117
3:1 81
3:6 . . . . 40, 41, 41n8, 82, 87
3:9 . . . . 41n8, 42
3:15 43
12:3 43
25:29–35 92
49:10 43
50:20 30

Exodus
16:1ff. 116
16:8 116
19 42
20:3 . . . . 45n9

Leviticus
10:3 164

Deuteronomy
5:24 42
29:29 118

Joshua
1:5 147

1 Samuel
3:13–14 163

2 Samuel
7:12–16 44

Psalms
3:4 26
16:1–2 102
16:10 44
16:11 159
19 69
19:1–2 38
19:7 . . . . 69, 70
19:8 70
19:10 70
34:6 26
51:4 53
55:12–14 151
55:16–17 26
56 . . . . 148n2
73:3 156
77:1 26
86:11 72
90:2 36
90:14 72
102:26 36
107:1 117
118 . . . . 148n2

119:15 73
119:16 73
119:18 72
119:27 73
119:36 72
119:68 117
119:97 73
135:6 114
142:1–3 26

Proverbs
9:10 82

Isaiah
7:14 44
42:8 . . . . .37, 120
48:11 120
53:4–12 44
53:9 44
53:11 44
55:8–9 120

Jeremiah
17:9 . . . . .93, 159
23:24 134

Lamentations
3:26 166

Jonah
4:4 164

Micah
5:2 44

Habakkuk
book of 57

Malachi
3:6 36

Matthew
1:22–23 44
5 74
5:13–14 148
5:28 91

5:45 74
6:9 75
6:9–10 156
6:12 53
6:14 53
6:25–43 126
6:27 116
8:14–17 75
9:35–37 155
10:39 104
12:34 26
16:24 99
25:41 54
26:69–72 100
27:46 125
28:19–20 154
28:19–21 130

Mark
1:40–45 . . . . .58n2
2 . . . . .154n8
2:1–13 . . . . .58n2
2:1–28 . . . . .58n2
2:9–11 . . . . .154n8
2:17 58
3:1–5 . . . . .58n2
5:1–43 . . . . .58n2
7:1–23 . . . . .58n2
8:34 99

Luke
9:23 . . . . .98, 99
12:6–7 115
15 44
15:1–7 44
15:8–10 44
15:13 44
15:22–24 44

John
4:34 105
8:29 105
8:58 36
14:17 48
14:20 48

14:23b 48
14:31.............37
15:5 103
15:20.............157
16:33.............121
17:3–4 105
17:13.............45
17:17.............68
17:23.............48
17:24.............36

Acts
book of 24, 55
2:22–23...........118
8.................55
8:1...............55
8:3...............55
16................54
16:19–24 24
16:24.............24
16:25.............24
17:7 149
17:25.............36

Romans
1:18–25...........98
1:21–23...........70
1:22–23...........41
1:25 ....41, 82, 88
3:9–18 55
3:10–12...........105
3:10–23...........105
3:12 101
3:23 ....53, 55
5:6–11 74
5:12 ....41n8
6.................108
6:18–19...........109
6:23 ....54, 105, 108
8:28 ....120, 126
8:32 127
11:34.............120

1 Corinthians
1:26–31...........132
3:1–6.............131

3:3...............131
3:18 70
15:45–48 133

2 Corinthians
3:18 69
4:4...............85
4:17 158
4:18 93
5:20 148
6:10 ....164, 165
12:10.............164

Galatians
1:6...............144
2:20 48
5.................91
5:19–21...........91
6:1–2.............154

Ephesians
1:5–6.............120
1:11 114
1:11–12...........120
1:21 134
1:22–23...........134
2.................91
2:1–3.............85, 92
2:12 159
4.................133
4:10 134
4:11–15...........131, 133
4:13 ....133, 134
4:15–16...........134
4:16 133
4:24 104

Philippians
2:14 26
3.................149
3:19 149
3:20–21...........149
4:4...............164
4:9–11 165
4:11 ....12, 22

4:11–12 . . . . .15, 25, 54, 113
4:12 . . . . .15, 165
4:13 . . . . .67, 68, 135, 150, 161

Colossians
1:20 155
1:21–22 44
2:13 53
2:14 127
3:1–4 13
3:5 109

1 Thessalonians
1:10 149
5:18 164

1 Timothy
1:15–16 55
3:1 91
4:8 66
6 . . . . .65, 68
6:5–6 66
6:7 68
6:9 68

2 Timothy
book of 143
3:16 143
3:17 69
4:2 143
4:3 143
4:3–4 143

Hebrews
book of 135, 140
2:1–4 137
3 . . . . .147n1
3:7–19 135
3:13 . . . . .139, 154
4:11 . . . . .147, 148
4:14–15 154
4:14–16 77
4:16 . . . . .76, 163

10 136
10:24 139
10:24–25 136
11:16 147
12:22 148
12:23 148
12:28 148
13 . . . . .12, 16, 147
13:5 . . . . .15, 114, 124, 147
13:5–6 . . . . .12, 16, 47
13:6 148
13:14 . . . . .148, 155, 156

James
1:2–4 122
1:3 62
1:13–15 . . . . .88, 108
1:17 118
5:7–8 61
5:10–11 62
5:11 62

1 Peter
1:3–6 154
1:8 46
3:18 . . . . .7, 98
4:12 157
5:7 26

1 John
book of 90, 96
1:3–4 45
2:15 . . . . .85, 95
2:16 . . . . .90, 91, 93
2:16–17 27
2:17 . . . . .93, 94, 95
3:4 53
4:8 36

Revelation
4:11 36
21–22 156